INDOOR GARDEN

INDOOR GARDEN

a new approach to growing and displaying plants in the
home and through the year with 300 practical photographs

DIANA YAKELEY

PHOTOGRAPHY BY CAROLINE ARBER

aquamarine

This book is for Nick and Lucy.

This edition is published by Aquamarine, an imprint of Anness Publishing Ltd, Hermes House, 88–89 Blackfriars Road, London SE1 8HA; tel. 020 7401 2077; fax 020 7633 9499

www.aquamarinebooks.com; www.annesspublishing.com

If you like the images in this book and would like to investigate using them for publishing, promotions or advertising, please visit our website www.practicalpictures.com for more information.

UK agent: The Manning Partnership Ltd; tel. 01225 478444; fax 01225 478440; sales@manning-partnership.co.uk

UK distributor: Grantham Book Services Ltd; tel. 01476 541080; fax 01476 541061; orders@gbs.tbs-ltd.co.uk

North American agent/distributor: National Book Network; tel. 301 459 3366; fax 301 429 5746; www.nbnbooks.com

Australian agent/distributor: Pan Macmillan Australia; tel. 1300 135 113; fax 1300 135 103; customer.service@macmillan.com.au

New Zealand agent/distributor: David Bateman Ltd; tel. (09) 415 7664; fax (09) 415 8892

A CIP catalogue record for this book is available from the British Library.

Publisher Joanna Lorenz
Managing Editor Judith Simons
Executive Editor Caroline Davison
Senior Art Manager Clare Reynolds
Designer Mark Latter
Photographer Caroline Arber
Stylist Charlotte Melling
Shoot Assistant Lisa Jones
Editorial Readers Richard McGinlay and Penelope Goodare
Production Controller Claire Rae

Ethical Trading Policy
Because of our ongoing ecological investment programme, you, as our customer, can have the pleasure and reassurance of knowing that a tree is being cultivated on your behalf to naturally replace the materials used to make the book you are holding. For further information about this scheme, go to www.annesspublishing.com/trees

Previously published as *Indoor Gardening*

page 1 Cress in little ceramic pots.

page 2 Sprouting daffodil (*Narcissus*) and grape hyacinth (*Muscari*) bulbs.

page 4 left: Bead plant (*Nertera granadensis*); centre: *Viola*; right: Ruby chard (*Beta vulgaris*).

page 5 left: Mind-your-own-business (*Soleirolia soleirolii*); centre: Blue glory bower (*Clerodendrum myricoides* 'Ugandense'); right: Kangaroo paw plant (*Anigozanthos flavidus*).

page 6 left: *Isolepsis cernua*; right: Hyacinths (*Hyacinthus orientalis*).

page 7 left: Mind-your-own-business (*Soleirolia soleirolii*); right: Ivy (*Hedera helix*).

contents

introduction	6	colour	70	practicalities	142
design points	8	seasonal displays	88	suppliers	156
interiors	28	edible plants	110	index	158
plant sculpture	56	plant focus	124	acknowledgements	160

introduction

As a small child I spent my pocket money on buying tiny plants and lined them up on my windowsill. They gave me great pleasure, impressed my parents and taught me about nature and nurture, responsibility and failure, and apparently cleaned the air in my bedroom at the same time. I sold the duplicates and offsets at the garden gate, which taught me the rudiments of commerce. What I did not consider at the time was the element of design needed to put the plants into a context, a place where they not only flourished, but formed part of a designed interior, too. Too much perhaps for a six-year-old.

The need to re-affirm our link with nature and to be surrounded with living plants is fundamental. The more we communicate through virtual reality and electronic data, the greater our need to touch base with real organic matter. The synergy between horticulture and street culture is evident through the number of style magazines that are aimed at a generation who are not traditionally interested in gardening and plants. Fashion now spills over into most aspects of design and there are new ways to combine clothes, homes and gardens. Handling plants seems to be a basic human desire and most rooms, however minimal, come alive with flowers and leaves to enhance them.

Today, there are numerous books on interiors and gardening, but there are few that combine the two, and that is what I hope to address in this book. Choosing the right container and position for your houseplant can elevate it to a piece of living sculpture, a work of art that draws the eye and complements the colours and textures of your home.

Successfully combining the plant, container and interior, as well as enhancing the colour scheme, is the art of indoor gardening. The mood and style of a room can be dramatically altered by the addition of a vibrantly coloured plant or a large architectural specimen. My own philosophy is to keep things simple. The contemporary interior is about space, light and reduction, with less clutter and larger areas of glass making it the perfect setting for well-chosen plants. Only specimen plants with sculptural lines will look right here, whereas the more traditional interior will happily absorb prettier, more rounded plants.

In the past, people treated the indoor plant as something that should go on forever and felt that to admit defeat with an ageing spider plant was tantamount to poisoning your granny. Many indoor plants have been forced in greenhouses and imported under unnatural conditions, and so will not last forever. But growing indoor plants is always better value than buying cut flowers, and when they are past their best either try propagating from them or throw them away. Nothing is more depressing than an unhealthy indoor plant. For this reason, discipline is important when shopping for plants. Impulse buys at garden centres should be avoided until you have worked out exactly where you wish to place the latest acquisition. An unsuitable position may be all right for a short time, but sooner or later it will take its toll. Given the right conditions, as well as proper care and attention, most indoor plants will flourish.

For me, plants have become an obsession and a therapy. Concentrating on these little miracles of nature will take your mind off the strains of modern living, provide visual delight, and enhance your environment at the same time. Quite a return on a relatively small investment.

design points

In an age where the prefix "designer" applies to almost everything, the indoor plant has somehow missed out. The successful combination of plant, pot and context rarely happens. With a little thought, all this can change.

scale and proportion

Designers draw plans to show how each part of a design will work, taking into account the space, light levels and function of the area. This is too much like hard work for indoor planting, but the same principles apply. Careful thought about size and position will create balance in an interior.

opposite, above and below These spectacular banana plants (*Musa*) help to create a smooth transition between the interior and the patio. The large, metallic pots subtly echo the metal floor grilles and door frames.

below Groups of objects can create an interesting arrangement. Green bamboo shoots, rooted in water in miniature vases and displayed inside tall glass holders, are arranged with exotic, green, spiky fruits.

First of all, stand back and look at your rooms, then ask yourself the following questions. Are the ceilings high or low? How much light comes into the room and when? Are there areas that need hiding or emphasizing? Once you have decided on these points, look at the proportions of the space and consider whether a big statement plant or a group of plants with a similar theme would look better.

Be bold with size and shape. The reason most indoor plants seem insignificant is because they are too small, overwhelmed by large furniture and high ceilings. Big and bold plants need space for their sculptural quality and architectural form to be fully appreciated. Remember that you will not be able to move large containers around too often, so ensure that the plants have enough light from the start. Large plants look best in spacious, contemporary, open-plan areas where the furniture has clean, spare lines and there is ample circulation space around the plant. Groups of similar pots with blocks of planting can also achieve this look. Imagine how stunning a square section of wild-flower meadow would look in a container on a dining table.

Small, charming arrangements work well in more intimate spaces. They also look wonderful if displayed in multiples to form a miniature indoor landscape. Rows of bamboo stems, sprouting acorns or avocado stones (pits) in individual glass containers are much more interesting than just one, and create the impression of a miniature laboratory.

Very large containers sometimes look best planted with low-growing, geometric plants topping the opening, the pot being dominant by its sheer size. In contrast, smaller plants can spill over the edges of their containers. These may be as simple as an egg cup or china bowl, the interest focusing on the delicate quality of the plant. As a rough guide, a two-thirds/one-third proportion works well. With a large pot, the one-third should be the planting, the two-thirds the container, while with smaller containers, two-thirds should be the planting and one-third the container. Rules are there to be broken, however, and, with a little practice, scale and proportion can be manipulated to great effect. Tiny plants grouped together *en masse* become a grand statement, while one large plant can look so perfectly proportioned in its space that it blends seamlessly with the interior.

style and placement

Most rooms tell a unique story about the lives of their owners: cool, modern, international jet-setter; eclectic, foreign traveller; young, urban professional; or comfortable country-dweller. Developing a design statement extends not only to the choice of furnishings and furniture, but also to the type of indoor plants. The designer's skill is then in selecting plants and pots that emphasize and complement the interior design and materials of the room, and so continue this personal theme.

Carefully study the room in question and decide whether it is formal or informal, classic or contemporary, rustic or urban chic, and then gauge whether the plant and container are in keeping with the style. If they are not, then the arrangement will never look right. For example, a sophisticated, white, minimal room needs nothing more than, say, a perfect white orchid in a precise glass container to emphasize the reduction of ornament and the purity of the space, whereas a country kitchen is the perfect place for a profusion of herbs in old terracotta pots. Both arrangements perfectly reflect the spirit of the room and reinforce the aesthetic of the interior design.

Once you have established the "look" you are trying to achieve, the question of positioning and grouping the containers becomes all-important. If there is a fireplace, it will form a natural focal point in the room and the mantelshelf is the perfect place for displaying a group of plants when the fire is not in use. If the fireplace is a long way from the window, then move the plants to a sunnier spot, or outside, for part of the time to recuperate.

Bookshelves, ledges and alcoves can all be beautifully enhanced with indoor plants, but it is perhaps the ubiquitous coffee table that can create the most impact, becoming the centre of attention with a crisp, low-level arrangement of plants and books. A grid arrangement of square containers planted with identical plants might look good here, as would a long low trough running the length of the table.

In general, plants look best grouped in odd numbers, that is in threes, fives and so on, but this is not a hard-and-fast rule. Indeed, a grid of even numbers that forms a single arrangement works brilliantly and creates the impression of a miniature indoor garden. Add objects with a similar shape or colour to the grouping in order to create a story about texture or form, or add a single cut bloom of the same hue or complexity.

above These delicate golden bamboos (*Phyllostachys aurea*) form a gentle living screen from the street, without blocking out the light. They could also be placed outdoors during the summer.

opposite A brightly lit alcove is the perfect spot for sun-loving purple basil (*Ocimum basilicum* 'Purple Ruffles'). Although plants usually look best grouped in odd numbers, using two pots and combining them with the vertical form of a simple vase is just right.

form and shape

Many of the plants included in this book have been chosen for their simple geometric form, their pared-down structure and the sense of balance they bring to a group of objects in a room. Strong form and shape is important in the modern, streamlined home.

Many of today's homes contain less clutter than ever before and allow more light to flood in. The popularity of white walls, wood or stone floors, as well as a few carefully chosen pieces of furniture is in tune with the celebrated German architect Mies van der Rohe's statement of the 1950s that "less is more". However, simply reducing the number of objects in an interior is not enough. Each piece in the room, including the indoor plants, must not only be of great beauty in its own right, but should complement the other pieces around it in order to form a harmonious whole.

A single flower or leaf in a vase can often have more impact than a whole bunch, allowing the eye to contemplate and appreciate the shape of the plant more easily. The importance of form applies also to the choice of indoor plants. A group of identical plants arranged together in order to create one geometric shape, such as a row of mind-your-own-business (*Soleirolia soleirolii*), may be chosen to echo another design element in the room and so strengthen the overall visual impact.

Getting the design right involves meticulous attention to detail, so that the end result looks effortlessly right. Rather than having a collection of mismatched plants and pots scattered haphazardly around the house, sit down and examine why they don't look as good as they could. It may be that the shape, character or colour of the plant bears no relation to the container or to the objects close by, let alone to the style of the home. For this reason, the arrangement will never sit easily in the room. Try sweeping everything off a shelf or windowsill and replacing all the objects with one perfect orchid or a starkly simple glass or Perspex container planted with a row of lustrous *Iris reticulata*. Then, just stand back and admire.

opposite The natural shape of these mind-your-own-business (*Soleirolia soleirolii*) suggests an indoor topiary display. The softly tactile foliage perfectly balances the severity of the fire surround.
below A Perspex container on a glass shelf provides a wonderful foil for the intense colour and complex form of these starkly beautiful *Iris reticulata*.

colour and scent

Two of the best attributes that plants can bring to an interior are those of colour and scent. A burst of colour in a neutral design scheme can change the whole balance of the room and create a real focal point. Match it with a hue in a painting or cushion, and create a subtly co-ordinated look.

top The sinuous form of a white moth orchid (*Phalaenopsis*) contrasts perfectly with the severe lines of this colourful piece of modern art.
above Lavender has a beautiful, relaxing scent, which can be enjoyed indoors for short periods of time.

We talk of colour in terms of temperature – red and yellow are warm, blue and green are cool. Different colours are also linked with different moods and emotions. White is calming, purifying and contemplative, while the fiery orange of, say, a bird-of-paradise (*Strelitzia reginae*) suggests South American heat and a fiery temperament. Think of the emotional impact of newly emerging crocuses after the grey of winter, the intimation of sunshine of that first spring narcissus and the spiritual uplift a fresh sharp green brings after a dusty day in the city. You can use colour to create various moods in your home. If you wish to create a harmonious design scheme, choose plants that have similar hues to your furnishings. To bring a touch of excitement and drama to a design, choose a plant with a strongly contrasting colour. The bright red *Guzmania lingulata*, for example, looks stunning against a wall in a strong, contrasting colour.

You can also use a combination of cut flowers and foliage plants to create different colour effects. For example, the purple-splashed foliage of *Gynura sarmentosa* looks intriguing next to the purplish-red and pink tones of a bunch of sweet peas. Beautiful combinations are endless once your eye is trained to see similarities of colour or texture. With the right pot, the end result can be a perfect still-life and very pleasing to the eye.

The seasons also have their colour associations. Spring brings the freshness of white, blue or pink hyacinths and lemon-yellow daffodils. Summer makes us think of hot pink bougainvillea and scarlet pelargoniums which, in turn, lead to the more muted shades of autumn and winter. Plants from all over the world are now available locally, and you can buy all kinds of exotica at any time of the year. It is, though, more pleasurable to work with the seasons.

The scent of flowers and foliage is an added bonus at any time of the year and can evoke powerful memories of childhood or special people, places and events. With the huge variety of plants now available from most garden centres and markets, it is possible to have year-round colour and scent from plants such as paper-white narcissi (*Narcissus papyraceus*), *Gardenia augusta*, jasmine (*Jasminum polyanthum*) and *Stephanotis floribunda*. The only roses suitable for use indoors are the miniature ones which come in a wonderful variety of colours, but, sadly, seem to have lost their scent with modern breeding methods. Spray them with your favourite perfume and cheat.

As well as the delightfully scented flowering plants, there is also a host of herbs that have the most evocative of scents, especially when brushed against. The fresh scent of mint (*Mentha*) and the warm Mediterranean bouquet of rosemary (*Rosmarinus*) add to the delicious aromas of a kitchen, while lavender has a powerful sleep-inducing fragrance, as well as wonderful mauve flowerheads and silvery grey foliage. Most herbs need high light levels and so a sunny kitchen windowsill is the best place to grow them.

above The delicate flowers of the paper-white narcissus (*Narcissus papyraceus*) have a powerful scent.
top left and right Try to suit the colour of a plant to its location. Here, the fiery red bracts of tropical *Guzmania lingulata* look stunning against a deep blue wall (left), while the pale blue flowers of *Clerodendrum myricoides* 'Ugandense' suit a soft yellow backdrop.

texture and pattern

Plants, particularly foliage plants, can add a richness of texture and pattern to the overall design of a room. The glorious intricacy of some leaves, stems and tendrils is a natural foil to the limited palette of colours and range of materials that is often found in the modern interior.

Many of the best houseplants are grown for their magnificent leaves, which often look like landscapes in their own right. Deep fissures and grooves, spots and veins, pleats and puckers, hairs and sticky bits, all add to the complex fascination of the plant. The gently ribbed leaves of a banana (*Musa*) instantly bring a tropical ambience to a living room, while the amazing fan-like pleats of the coconut palm (*Cocos nucifera*) or the delicate tracery of a miniature bamboo conjure up images of the Far East. Interesting textures invite you to reach out and touch them. It is hard to resist patting the wonderful mounds of *Soleirolia soleirolii*, the mind-your-own-business plant, while the translucent beauty of *Sparrmannia africana* when light shines through its pale, downy leaves is breathtaking.

Succulents, with their amazing ability to store moisture, display particularly varied textures and patterns. The elegant, magisterial *Aeonium* 'Zwartkop' has smooth, shiny black rosettes, while the echeverias have soft, matt greeny blue foliage that looks wonderfully modern in a metal container (although their petal-like delicacy would look equally at home in a traditional interior). Members of the large *Kalanchoe* family provide colour, form and texture, and positively thrive on neglect. The fleshy leaves are often tipped with subtle colour, particularly *K. thyrsiflora* whose pale green leaves are tinged with red and covered in a soft bloom. But, of the succulents, perhaps the ultimate in minimalism are the living stones (*Lithops*). With their pairs of fat fleshy leaves, which part to allow through a flower, they have a science-fiction air about them.

opposite, top Blue-grey slate top-dresses this zinc container to create a crunchy contrast with the smooth, lush greenery of a banana (*Musa*).
opposite, bottom A visual pun on stones, both living and long dead. Living stones (*Lithops*), a type of succulent, and a collection of real stones and fossils create a miniature landscape of contrasting textures. The marble dish on a worn travertine table completes the picture.
left The geometric precision of this display is echoed in the mathematical complexity of the succulents, although their rosette-like structure brings some softness to the grid.
below The leaves of this variegated pelargonium have colour, texture and form. There is no need for flowers.

Even the simple addition of a mulch or top-dressing can give an arrangement added texture, setting off the plant to perfection, while also helping to retain moisture. Indeed, some of the more subtle plants look better displayed against a background of white gravel or crushed shell. A layer of sand beneath a cactus suggests a mini desert, while sea shells are reminiscent of summer at the beach. Paying attention to the finishing touches in this way will ensure your displays look well designed.

We are all familiar with the irregular patterning of begonia and pelargonium leaves, but for a truly weird experience look to carnivorous plants, such as pitcher plants (*Sarracenia*) and Venus flytraps (*Dionaea muscipula*), for their intricate form, grasping little claws or juicy pitcher-shaped flytraps. They need either rainwater or filtered, lime-free tap water as heavily chlorinated water will kill them. The markings on pitcher plants are strangely beautiful and often richly variegated. They live on flying insects and are the most eco-friendly way of keeping flying pests at bay.

containers

Choosing good containers is vitally important. A collection of square, round and rectangular containers in different materials is a great starting point. Plain containers suit both urban and rural interiors and will not detract from the impact of the plant.

opposite, top left A simple, glazed, white pot contrasts in colour and texture with the black slate labels.

opposite, top right Old terracotta pots have an enduring appeal and are perfect for collections of herbs and bulbs.

opposite, bottom left These cast-aluminium pots are a modern take on the terracotta ones, and are ideal for herbs.

opposite, bottom right Scaled down versions of gardening tools can be both practical and attractive. Having the right tools for the job is immensely satisfying.

below These pale lavender *Primula obconica* have a fresh country air and are planted in just the right container, a contemporary grass basket.

Build up a collection of simple graphic shapes in materials such as glass, metal and stone in various heights and sizes. Long, low containers look wonderful on a mantelshelf or hall table, while softer, more rounded containers might be more suitable for a bedside table. Perspex or glass containers are good for seeing the roots of spring bulbs as they grow. Different materials create different moods. Concrete and metal look urban and edgy, terracotta and ceramic more gentle and rustic. Baskets lined with plastic sheeting have a more traditional feel and look good with spring or autumnal arrangements.

Rough-textured pots in materials such as concrete look wonderful with succulent plants, and suggest the sort of dry rough landscape from which these specimens originate. With glass containers, drop the potted plant inside and fill the void at the sides with pebbles or slate chippings, moss or gravel – in fact, anything small and interesting that will give an extra design dimension. Sea shells, fir cones, buttons...the list is as unlimited as your imagination.

Both container and arrangement should relate to the design of the room. Strong angular furniture in a modern, loft-style apartment needs strong architectural displays to reinforce the design, whereas soft and sensual planting in a romantic bedroom makes for a relaxing atmosphere. Kitchens are where many people eat and socialize, so including a few indoor plants is a must. The kitchen should also offer

up a wealth of containers, including bowls, stainless-steel pans and buckets. A layer of gravel or pieces of polystyrene in the base of the pan will provide drainage and judicious watering should keep the plant quite happy.

With many people now working from home, there is often a study or home office where plants can play a role. Containers should be crisp and business-like or perhaps add a splash of colour to an otherwise monochrome scheme. When working on computer screens, it is advisable to rest your eyes for a few moments every twenty minutes or so. What better to rest them on than a beautiful plant or group of plants?

Shopping for pots can be as much fun as searching for plants. Old farm pails and bins are currently in favour in smart florists' shops, while chicken feeders can even be used as original window boxes. Auction sales can be a source of very original containers, and many delightful pieces can be found, cleaned and polished, and then added to the appropriate interior.

Some pots come with their own matching water tray, but standing a pot within a decorative container usually looks better. It is very important to check regularly that water is not building up in the base, as this could lead to mildew and stale smells.

different containers

1 Birch bark container
Lined with a plastic sheet

2 Tiny terracotta pots
Ideal for growing cacti

3 Small tin containers
Useful as table decorations

4 Old terracotta pots
Perfect for a rustic look

5 Recycled fibre pots
Ideal for growing seedlings

6 Simple terracotta pots
Good for a modern look

7 Ceramic container
Perfect for a contemporary
display

8 Tapered metal pots
For multiple arrangements

9 Heavy metal basket
Ideal for hiding a pot with a
saucer inside

10 Thin porcelain pots
Useful as table decorations

11 Cheerful china pots
Ideally come with their own
saucer to sit on

12 Inexpensive oval tin
Sits well on shelves
or windowsills

13 Night-light holders
Fun to use for growing
mustard and cress or for
tiny cuttings

14 White curvy container
Ideal for flowering plants,
perhaps in a bedroom

15 Perspex office pots
Make excellent plant
containers, although they
have no drainage holes

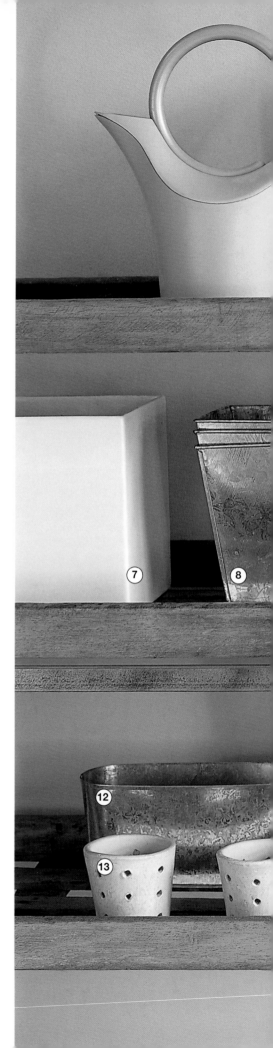

tools and accessories

Once the pleasures of indoor gardening have taken hold, you will need an assortment of tools and accessories to help you keep the arrangements in pristine condition. Using the smartest implements, you will soon find that tending your plants is as rewarding as admiring them.

top An elegant modern watering can will make watering your plants a pleasure, rather than a chore.
above Tie bundles of twigs with string in order to make decorative additions to winter plant arrangements.
opposite The luxury of an indoor potting area adds to the therapy of handling and growing plants.

One of the most important items in your indoor gardening toolkit is a pair of gardening gloves, especially for handling prickly cacti. It is nice to have a pair specifically for working indoors on your potted plants. A collection of plant labels in different materials, such as slate and wood, is also invaluable, making the process of identifying your plants so much more enjoyable than with ugly plastic labels. It is possible to find long-handled, miniature versions of garden trowels and forks to make digging around in a small pot a great deal easier. Of course, it is just as good to use old kitchen spoons and forks, but not nearly so stylish.

Sometimes string or wire is needed to anchor the wayward stems of truly vigorous plants. Indeed, perhaps one of life's great pleasures is to be given a big ball of string, both for the tarry smell and for the intricate structure created by the manufacture of the ball – simple, useful and entirely satisfactory.

A watering can with a long spout is useful for reaching between leaves and directing the water to where you want it to be rather than bouncing off the leaves on to the cream silk cover next to them. There are so many well-designed modern watering cans available that they are just too good to put away. A fine pump-action mister is also useful because moisture is absorbed through the leaves of plants and it also helps to keep dust from dulling them.

Your plants may do so well that they need support as they grow. Canes and stakes are strong and practical but don't always look good. So, collect interesting branches on country walks (sometimes with the added bonus of lichen) and use these. Birch twigs pushed into the potting mix in a container, perhaps planted with paper-white narcissi (*Narcissus papyraceus*)

or hellebores with their nodding flowers, both support the fragile stems and enhance the composition, suggesting a natural woodland setting. Colourful chopsticks can also make elegant supports for smaller plants, while reeds soaked in water can be used to make interesting shapes and horizontal supports, rather like basket-making. If you are able to find old pieces of vine root, or beautiful tree bark, then these could make useful additions to an orchid arrangement. Once you start looking, all kinds of oddments will suggest a use in your planting scheme.

Never throw away broken terracotta pots; just break them up into small pieces to use as crocks for drainage at the bottom of another pot. Try to keep everything spotlessly clean both to prevent cross infection of bugs and viruses and because it looks so much more attractive. If you are lucky enough to have a special area for all your indoor-gardening tasks, so much the better.

Experiment with a wide collection of different decorative mulches and top-dressings. They can be stored in other pots or glass jars for easy access, and will add a finishing touch to your plant arrangements. A top-dressing of rich green moss would suit a more traditional display in a terracotta pot, but there are also other more modern mulches to choose from, including buttons, shells, fossils, pebbles, stones, coloured gravel, crushed glass, metal-coated pellets and even dried starfish.

top A ball of string and some beech plant labels are both decorative and useful.
above Keep spare decorative mulches in tiny metal buckets or glass jars.

decorative mulches

1 Silver pellets
For modern plant displays in a minimal interior

2 Spanish moss
Ideal for giving texture and interest to a display

3 White pebbles
Smart and clean, perfect for an all-white scheme

4 Dried starfish
Perfect for a plant display in a bathroom

5 Fine grit
Ideal for top-dressing cacti and succulents

6 Bun moss
Traditional top-dressing that looks good with terracotta

7 Buttons
Suit a display of flowering plants in a bedroom

8 Black pebbles
Perfect for a study in black and white

9 Crushed shells
Delicate and pretty, perfect for cacti and succulents

interiors

Plants enhance every part of the house, but, in terms of ideal growing conditions, some rooms will present a challenge. With flair and a little know-how, even the darkest hallway or bathroom can play host to some greenery.

living rooms

Living rooms tend to be warmer and drier than other rooms, and often have a greater ratio of windows to floor area. This is ideal for most houseplants, but not for those that need a cooler site, so care needs to be taken with plant choice. Shade- and damp-loving plants need not apply.

below and opposite Sprouted wheat grass (*Elymus*) makes for an unexpectedly sophisticated arrangement in the right container. White stones are used to disguise the bare soil. The linear and precise design of both the table and sofa are mirrored in the clipped cushions of wheat grass and white stones. This is a perfect minimal garden.

The living room is quite often the room in the house on which you spend the most money and thought. So, it is important to choose the right plants in order to complete the picture. Well-chosen plants can lead the eye to a particular piece of furniture or group of objects, co-ordinating the colours or textures. Play shapes and colours off against one another for further interest or add height with a large specimen plant to a corner of a room in which most of the furniture is at a fairly uniformly low level.

Many homes have rooms that combine dining, cooking and relaxing in one open-plan space. In such an area, bold architectural plants would go well with the strong, clean lines of modern furniture. It is better to spend more on one or two truly wonderful mature specimen plants with a good shape and habit than to have a number of smaller plants dotted around the house. A single specimen can look dramatic or two specimens can be used, placed either side of a doorway - perhaps one leading outside. Large single specimen plants can also look impressive silhouetted against a window. Take care when the temperature outside falls too low because few plants can take both heat and extremes of cold and draught. Frequent misting is advisable if the room is hot and dry.

The choice of plants for a living room should be guided by the decor. The powerful verdancy of the tray of wheat grass (*Elymus*) and white stones shown here

reflects the style of the room and provides a focal point in an otherwise neutral, white interior, but, perhaps most important of all, it does not impede circulation around the table. Indeed, with heavily trafficked areas, it is better to have plants that do not intrude into the space too much as they will be constantly bruised and battered. Juiced, wheat grass is said to be a great cure for hangovers and research is ongoing into its other curative properties. Kept clipped and watered, it will keep fresh for several weeks before it needs replacing with freshly sprouted wheat grains.

In a more traditional, less open-plan home, the living room may also be the most formal room in the house – a quiet spot for reading books and magazines or a place for entertaining. This calls for more elegant, formal arrangements, such as roses or lilies planted in geometric containers or smaller, neat glass or ceramic pots filled with seasonal bulbs positioned on either side of sofas.

For many people the living area is used only at night after a day's work and, during the autumn and winter, it is also often only seen in artificial light. If you have adjustable downlights, try tilting one to highlight a particular specimen plant and, for further dramatic effect, dim the lights elsewhere. Lighting the plant from below a glass table can also be very effective and is especially good if the container is particularly interesting or is made from a reflective material.

Choosing container shapes and styles that relate to the furnishing style of the room immediately suggests a good eye for the details of design. The crisp white container shown on this page, planted with *Primula* Gold-laced Group, is a perfect match for the geometric shape of the table. It also sets off to great effect the complexity of what is often considered to be a rather old-fashioned plant. The arrangement is perfect for this modern living space, looking fresh and appealing as well as echoing the rich colours of the sofa cushions.

above and opposite *Primula* Gold-laced Group provides a focal point of colour and looks surprisingly contemporary planted in a white ceramic container. The container is perfectly matched to its modern surroundings, with the primulas toning beautifully with the cushions and books – which provide the only other splashes of colour in this serene living area.

dining rooms

The concept of having a separate room for dining is fast becoming a thing of the past. Those who cook usually like to converse with their guests and the dining table also tends to be the hub of family life. Often, the dining room has to double up as a work room or office. However, it is difficult to resist the urge to place a few plants on such a large area of space, and they can be witty and decorative additions to seasonal or festive meals.

Indoor plant displays for the dining room may be formal or informal. A display of gardenias, with their compact shape, glossy leaves and wonderful fragrance, is a particularly good choice for a formal dining-table arrangement. Planted in polished aluminium pots, they look very smart, matching the gleaming, stainless-steel cutlery and newly starched white linen. The result is simple, elegant and fresh, while also leaving enough space to accommodate a plethora of serving dishes and flickering candles for a celebration dinner. A beautifully presented dining table, such as this, suggests fine attention to detail as well as a real love for all the good things in life.

Pleasing and evocative effects can also be produced by decorating the table with pots of edible plants in order to forge a link with the food. Small pots of herbs can look delightful, provided the pots are spotlessly clean, and the plants are healthy and have a good shape. Mat-forming Corsican mint (*Mentha requienii*), for example, makes a pungent dining-table decoration, while very small bay, citrus or rosemary plants suggest Mediterranean meals under the sun. Although strictly a garden plant, rosemary (*Rosmarinus officinalis*) is a highly aromatic evergreen herb that makes an attractive occasional visitor indoors. Some suppliers sell miniature fruiting olive trees in old terracotta pots. These too would look wonderful marching down the centre of an old pine table for a relaxed Sunday lunch with friends and family, conjuring up memories of shared holidays and good simple food.

In general, planting should be kept to a low level so that it does not obscure your vision across the table. A low-level plant at each place setting can be both charming and practical. Herbs such as thyme, with their compact habit and association with delicious smells and tastes, are

opposite, left and below A simple, silver-and-white theme is perfect for a celebratory meal at home. The plant arrangements do not obstruct the view across the table, while *Gardenia augusta* 'Veitchiana' adds a delicious scent to the air. Just before the meal, tie fresh gardenia leaves to a white linen napkin with knotted blades of grass. The shiny, dark green leaves of the gardenias are the perfect foil for the rose-like white flowers. The polished aluminium pots are a modern version of a traditional flower pot shape.

ideal candidates for this treatment. Other small, clump-forming plants, such as mind-your-own-business (*Soleirolia soleirolii*), with its delicate froth of tiny leaves, or the bright orange bead plant (*Nertera granadensis*), would be just as suitable, although the latter two are not edible. Even cress and mustard, grown in tiny egg cups or tea-light holders, can be charming and humorous. Mixed with groups of identically coloured fruit, such as lemons, apples or kiwi fruit, the effect is graphic and enticing.

For a seasonally themed dinner party, you might wish to arrange small terracotta flowerpots planted with club moss (*Selaginella*), which is reminiscent of a woodland floor, and thyme along the table. Use seed labels written with felt-tipped pens for the place names and then strew the table with fresh seasonal berries – blackberries in autumn, for example, would be wonderful. Each place setting could be decorated with a little bowl of home-produced mushrooms. These can be grown easily indoors, the beautiful oyster variety needing only a couple of toilet rolls, a warm place and a refrigerator in order to produce a crop. Button (white) mushrooms can also be grown indoors and there is nothing better than producing a basket of these fascinating crops. There are many mushroom-growing kits available by mail order.

Indoor plants on dining tables should obviously be kept in pristine condition. You don't really want to be looking at potting mix while eating or entertaining. An excellent idea for embellishing a dining-table display is to use small fruits or nuts as a decorative mulch. For example, bright orange kumquats look brilliant placed under sprouting spring bulbs. In autumn and winter, you might like to try using dried kidney beans, lentils or walnuts in their shells. Organic top-dressings should be removed from the surface of the pot before they begin to rot.

above Even a simple meal of bread and cheese can be elevated to a lazy, Mediterranean-style lunch in the sunshine by the addition of a fragrant rosemary (*Rosmarinus officinalis*) and an evocative lemon plant (*Citrus limon*).
opposite An autumnal country lunch party, with Corsican mint (*Mentha requienii*) in pots and hedgerow blackberries linking matching pots filled with club moss (*Selaginella*) down the centre of the table. The arrangement suggests a fresh seasonal menu.

kitchens

Every gardener will want to include plants in the kitchen. The preparation and presentation of food are enhanced by the addition of a few fresh leaves, so a selection of herbs on the windowsill is an obvious choice. However, there are also decorative indoor plants that will add interest to the kitchen.

It is difficult to resist having some indoor plants on your kitchen windowsill, whether they are edible plants, such as herbs and salad leaves, or purely decorative. It just seems to be the right place for sprouting pips and seeds, rooting some broken sedum baby or growing some fiery chilli peppers. Kitchens are warm and steamy, and you can observe the progress (or lack of it) of your plants while doing some other task.

The ease of snipping the youngest, most succulent, mixed salad leaves from a window box and throwing them into a salad bowl in six seconds takes some beating. If you grow cut-and-come-again varieties, you can just cut what you need, rather than harvesting a whole lettuce, and you can also sow more seed as spaces appear in the container. In this way, you will have a constant supply of fresh salad leaves that you have grown yourself. You can buy packets of mixed seed from many suppliers so that you can have a good selection of different leaves for a summer salad. Another attractive alternative to a window box of salad leaves would be to grow some ruby or rhubarb chard (*Beta vulgaris*) on a kitchen window ledge. Grown in an old terracotta pot, it would look spectacular with the light shining through the leaves.

Rhubarb (*Rheum × hybridum*) is another leafy edible plant that looks wonderful with the light streaming in behind it. It is particularly spectacular when young and compact. The bright green leaves, which are

above left The delicate leaves of ruby chard seedlings (*Beta vulgaris*) look perfect on a sunny kitchen window ledge.
left Simple shapes and materials create a pleasing still-life, with sunflowers and young salad seedlings in a rural kitchen.

opposite All the accessories in this kitchen come together to suggest that the owner enjoys cooking. Sunshine streams through cut-and-come-again salad leaves and the cut stems of clover are perfectly placed in a sensuously shaped enamel jug.

horribly poisonous, have complex veining and intricately curled edges, but it is the deep red stalks that are the edible part. Planted in a large, metal, kitchen pot, rhubarb makes a gently humorous statement. It is, strictly speaking, a garden resident, so it should be planted out in the garden (where it will eventually grow nearly big enough for you to hide under), but there is something very rewarding about growing an outdoor plant inside for a few weeks. The arrangement would need no decorative mulch as a finishing touch, just a rich, earthy potting mix to suggest a kitchen garden.

For a more decorative, modern look, why not grow some pretty pot marigolds (*Calendula officinalis*), both for their charming simplicity and to sprinkle the petals over a salad for an unexpected burst of colour? Lined up in identical metal pots on a kitchen worktop, they look fresh and clean in a contemporary space.

A useful addition to the ever-expanding windowsill is the elegant *Aloe vera*. With its stark sculptural shape, it is reminiscent of the desert and is possibly the only plant suitable for the most minimal of kitchens. Aloe vera gel, which is extracted from the leaf, can be applied externally to promote the healing of cuts, burns, sunburn, eczema and skin irritation, to name just a few of its wonderful medicinal properties. In the commercial production of aloe vera gel, the leaves are cut and the sap is used fresh, preserved and bottled or dried to a brown crystalline solid for use in creams, lotions and medicinal preparations. In the home, you can rub the sap on to those inevitable agave lacerations and invisible cactus punctures in the skin on your hands.

above Using kitchen containers for edible plants is a gentle visual pun. Rhubarb can be grown indoors in a large container for a short time, but should then be planted in the garden.

opposite Pot marigolds (*Calendula officinalis*) have a charming simplicity and can be lined up in identical metal pots in a kitchen. The bright orange petals can be sprinkled over a salad.

bedrooms

Although many modern bedrooms have built-in storage and contain little else but a bed and perhaps a small bedside table, you should not let this restrict your choice of indoor plants for this room. If space is a problem, then the most practical choice is an interesting selection of small, compact plant arrangements.

Pots of sprouting spring bulbs are fresh and spare, and have the added advantage of producing a delicious scent, while simple bowls of white or cream miniature roses would be perfect in an all-white bedroom, sensuous and pure at the same time. Complete the design with the finest crisp, white bed linen and armfuls of scented white cut flowers.

Orchids, such as moth orchids (*Phalaenopsis*) and slipper orchids (*Paphiopedilum*), look just right in a bedroom. They come in a variety of different colours, which you can harmonize with the colour scheme of your room. You could place a white orchid, for example, near some black-and-white photographs of flowers, allowing the graphic quality of both to create a wonderfully strong combination.

Lavender has sleep-inducing properties, as well as being a pleasing colour for a bedroom. It needs warm sunlight, though, so it is best saved for a short visit to the bedroom before going back to the garden. Cut some flowerheads to put under your pillow for a serene night's sleep. Similarly, the soft blue of a Cape leadwort (*Plumbago auriculata*) would look stunning in a bedroom window or climbing in from a sheltered balcony, but it really needs a conservatory (sun room) and so is a perfect visitor for a guest bedroom over a few days.

left The contrasting textures of suede and leather, fur and linen in neutral colours make for a tactile and sensuous bedroom, further enhanced by the amazing orchid, *Paphiopedilum parishii*, in its birch-bark container.

Bedrooms that have lots of surfaces, such as chests of drawers, dressing tables or even perhaps a little table next to a comfortable chair for reading, are perfect for a few indoor plants. Link the colour of the flowers to the colour of the soft furnishings. Be bold and create a sense of theatre with an ornate and decadent antique bed matched with the mysterious, nocturnal-looking flowerhead of the devil flower (*Tacca chantrieri*).

A softly curved container planted with a pretty flowering plant would work well in a bedroom, whether you choose the delicate beauty of an iris or cyclamen, the frilly flowers of eustoma or the bolder velvety delights of a bowl of pansies (*Viola*). Choose from the drama of the near-black *V.* 'Molly Sanderson' or the intense blue of some of the other varieties or just a wonderful patchwork of colour from a packet of mixed seeds. Pansies are available in a variety of colours, so opt for a single hue or a mixture of different shades for a more riotous effect.

above A *Campanula isophylla* in a curvaceous pot is top-dressed with tiny mother-of-pearl buttons. It looks ultra-feminine in this all-white bedroom.
right The amethyst colours of these lovely hellebores (*Helleborus*) tone perfectly with the bedcovers and cushions in a comfortable bedroom. Hellebores are, strictly speaking, garden plants, enjoying cold conditions, but they can be brought indoors for a few days to decorate a guest bedroom.
opposite A flower-strewn, satin- and silk-upholstered French bed, combined with a curvy, flesh-pink pot, creates an air of decadence. The truly exotic bat or devil flower (*Tacca chantrieri*) has something of the night about it too.

bathrooms

Bathrooms are for relaxing and unwinding. Imagine candles, a glass of chilled wine, a scented bath oil, and luxuriously soft, fluffy towels for the ultimate bathing experience – soothing, sensual and relaxing after a day in a grey city. Lush greenery is the obvious choice for these watery havens.

For most people, splashing around in water is an invigorating or calming pastime, as well as a refreshing necessity. Many plants enjoy the same watery pleasures, and what could be better than some organic greenery on a bathroom shelf or windowsill?

Plants with a good form and shape are ideal for a bathroom. Miniature bamboos look crisp, clean and contemporary in a row of identical containers. These bamboos love to be damp, and look suitably Zen-like in a modern bathroom, especially if a container can be found that suggests the Far East or relates in some way to the materials used in the bathroom.

Ferns and aquatic plants enjoy the damp air in a bathroom. Ferns are happy in fairly low light levels and most love to be damp and misted, their delicate fronds making a perfect foil to a tiled room. There are a huge number of varieties to choose from, including the glossy-leaved aspleniums and the hard fern (*Blechnum gibbum*) with its uncurling fronds. Aquatic plants, such as the umbrella plant (*Cyperus involucratus*), need their feet in water at all times, but are quite happy in the corner of a bathroom. The stems are easily bent, so snip off any offending tufts.

above This limestone and glass bathroom has a Zen-like simplicity which is echoed in the miniature bamboos in concrete containers. **left** Enjoying a soak, these hard ferns (*Blechnum gibbum*) look just right with Victorian taps and an old-fashioned sink.

opposite The umbrella plant (*Cyperus involucratus*) is very happy in this moist bathroom. It is set off beautifully by the green walls. Needing to have its feet in water, a bathroom is the perfect room for growing this plant.

hallways

Most hallways are relatively dark, narrow and draughty, with a radiator – not the ideal place for growing indoor plants. However, the hallway is the room where first impressions are made, so do keep some plants here, but choose types that will thrive in less than perfect conditions.

To enhance the less than showy plants that will survive in a dark hallway, use interesting or colourful containers. Where the container is the main interest in terms of shape and form, the plant can play a less important role. You will also need to make sure that the containers are not too unsteady, however, as this is a room where coats are removed and umbrellas shaken.

If you want brightly coloured flowering plants, you may have to accept that, after a few weeks, they will have to be moved to a more suitable situation or back into the garden. Rooted plants are better value than cut flowers in terms of longevity, but may have been forced in unnatural conditions and so will not last forever, no matter how hard you try.

The plants you can grow in the hallway will obviously depend on how much space there is. If you are fortunate enough to have a large hall, with top light from windows around the staircase, grow large architectural specimens that can use the height of the stairwell to great advantage, growing up between the floors. If your hallway is rather small, make use of the stairs themselves. A row of plants marching up the stairs is fun, but choose compact plants such as the soft plump mounds of mind-your-own-business (*Soleirolia soleirolii*) or club moss (*Selaginella*).

The hallway is also a link with the outside and, sometimes, small specimen trees such as privet (*Ligustrum*) can be moved from the doorstep for brief periods of time. During periods of intense cold, outdoor plants can also overwinter here, but make sure that the heat does not dry out the roots.

above The architectural purity of this stairway is complemented by mounds of mind-your-own-business (*Soleirolia soleirolii*) in handmade Japanese bowls.
opposite The indoor-outdoor look is perfect for the transitional space between a living area and the outside. Privet (*Ligustrum*) standards in smart zinc planters look equally at home on the outside porch or in the hallway.

home offices

With the advent of modern communications, many people do some of their work from home, and most homes need an area for filing documents and using a computer. Where space is at a premium, the living room may have an area dedicated to these tasks. If you incorporate an office area into a living space, it should ideally be planned into the layout at an early stage and then built in to a recess so that doors can be closed across the work area when it is time to relax or entertain.

Electronic office equipment, such as faxes and printers, can look unattractive, so this is an ideal situation for a few plants to create some colour, texture and, if possible, scent, although too much would be a distraction. Studies by NASA show that an efficient way to counteract the harmful chemicals emitted by synthetic furnishings, cleaning materials and electrical equipment is to grow plants indoors.

As most worktops are needed for paperwork, it is better to choose neat plants that do not spread all over the place and drop leaves or need to be supported or tied in. The bead plant (*Nertera granadensis*), with its bright orange berries like little beads or lentils, is deliciously compact. Several small plants in a long, narrow container make a graphic splash of colour and, provided they are kept moist, will last for months. Spring bulb displays can also lift the spirits and add colour and scent. Planted in modern containers with clean lines and a crisp top-dressing, they will last well and dispel winter blues.

Most succulent plants are happy in an office, provided that there is plenty of light. Their graphic shapes enhance the working atmosphere. Choose plants that will inspire creative thought with their beautifully intricate form or complex flower structure.

above right Muscular, graphic furniture and forms are in keeping with the urban live/work space in a converted, loft-style apartment. The concrete seat, stone planter and a smart bicycle look perfect with the clean lines and architectural form of a magnificent specimen of *Agave americana*.

opposite and right The odd little bead plant (*Nertera granadensis*) looks just right in an office space. It is neat and business-like planted *en masse* in a long metal container on top of a desk. The colour of the plants works well with the greys, oranges and whites of the office accessories.

conservatories

In a cooler climate, the ultimate space for the indoor gardener is the conservatory (sun room). Plants that would not survive in darker rooms indoors will thrive here, enjoying the higher light levels. You can control the conditions to provide just the right environment for your plants.

opposite A traditional conservatory makes a delightful summer dining room and, if heated, it can be used all year round in a cool climate. Softly coloured paintwork and cream stone floors make for a relaxing and contemplative space.
right *Mandevilla* x *amoena* 'Alice du Pont'. is a magnificent twining climber for the conservatory. It has blowsy, funnel-shaped, pink flowers and dark green leaves.
below The hot pink, petal-like bracts of bougainvillea surround insignificant white flowers.

A visit to a local botanic garden will show that different plants will grow in varying levels of heat and humidity. In a cool conservatory with a temperature of about 2°C (36°F), you can overwinter tender garden plants, such as fuchsias and pelargoniums, as well as grow more exotic plants, including climbers such as Cape leadwort (*Plumbago*), passion flower (*Passiflora*), jasmine (*Jasminum*) and edible grapes (*Vitis*). A warm conservatory in which the temperature does not drop below 7°C (45°F), remaining warm but not too humid or too dry, is perfect for most Mediterranean plants, such as bougainvilleas and citrus trees. The hot conservatory, with a minimum temperature of around 20°C (68°F) and high humidity, is suitable for truly exotic plants that originate from tropical regions. These include banana plants, bromeliads, exotic ferns and orchids as well as the wonderful glory lily (*Gloriosa superba*), a glossy leaved climber with complex and dramatic, bright yellow or red flowers, which change to dark orange or deep red.

A conservatory is the ideal place to grow large-scale plants such as climbers and trailers that you could not grow within the confines of your home. You can create a lush, tropical atmosphere with swathes of wonderfully fragrant and colourful blossom. They can be easily supported by fixed wires and vine eyes, which is not usually an option in living areas.

Where space is limited, climbers can be tied in to a framework or hoop of wire. Plants such as a mauve-blue *Clerodendrum*, the pure white *Stephanotis floribunda* and the scented jasmine (*Jasminum polyanthum*) come from the nursery already trained in this way. Ideal for conservatory tables and staging, they have the added advantage of a heady perfume and purity of colour. Where there is ample space and light, let them cascade or climb more naturally.

There are some practical points to bear in mind when growing plants in a conservatory. You will need various forms of heat and light control, as well as some form of humidity control. Good ventilation is another important factor. This can be regulated by automatic openers and fans, otherwise the manual opening of doors and windows is essential to prevent a build-up of heat or damp. A few hours of uncontrolled strong sun beating down on glass can damage delicate leaves, as can a few hours of frost, so you will need to provide some kind of shading, and use a good thermometer to check on the temperature and take action accordingly. Constantly check for signs of insect damage and deal with the offenders immediately. Find out from your local nursery about biological controls for various pests and diseases because you will not want to sit and eat under a chemical cloud of poisonous substances. If possible, you should also keep a tank of rainwater in the conservatory, both to keep up the humidity and to water the plants easily.

opposite The humble white busy Lizzie, *Impatiens* New Guinea Group, makes a chic arrangement when massed in a linear, metal window box.

above right Osteospermums, with their magenta flowers, create a splash of colour on a window ledge. The glazed pots have their own matching saucers, which makes all the difference on polished surfaces.

right Cape leadwort (*Plumbago auriculata*) is an evergreen climber from South Africa with clusters of pale blue flowers. There is also a white variety, *P. auriculata* var *alba*. It will need cutting back as it can be vigorous.

plant sculpture

Many indoor plants have a strong architectural form and their bold, powerful shapes can be used to define and complement a range of contemporary interiors.

architectural plants

If plants are to make a positive addition to an interior, they should be compatible with the space in terms of size and shape. Plants with a strong form and shape can make a dramatic impact on a room, becoming a piece of sculpture in their own right.

above The scale and proportion of the plant and container are well matched here with the magnificent form of an *Agave americana* in a simple white pot dressed with white stones. Pure, strong, graphic and immensely pleasing.
opposite Light pouring through the soft green leaves of African hemp (*Sparrmannia africana*) reveals the delicate tracery of veins and shows off the structural form very well.

Modern architecture creates free-flowing spaces with large expanses of light, thus reducing unnecessary elements and creating a sense of calm. The plants that are most suited to this type of space are those whose strong form and leaf structure are the main interest, rather than an intricate flower. The pot, too, must have strong, simple lines to complement both the plant and the surrounding architecture.

A large specimen bush that looks wonderful in a room with a high ceiling and plenty of light is the African hemp (*Sparrmannia africana*). It is perfect for standing on a table to give a vertical element to a room. The huge downy leaves look ethereal with light shining behind them, while the lime-green colour looks fresh throughout the year. Always water with rainwater, or at least not with hard water, to avoid brown blotches. The Canary date palm (*Phoenix canariensis*), a classic indoor plant that will flourish if it has plenty of light, has elegant, arching fronds that create a striking focal point in a large, plain white container. Another architectural group of plants, *Dracaena*, contains many species of palm-like plants from Africa and Asia. They create the impression of an exotic plant, while actually being quite tough. This has made them very popular indoor plants. Dracaenas rely on simple but very striking variegation and a bold outline for their attraction. *D. marginata* 'Tricolor' is particularly striking, with green, cream and red striped leaves.

The sculptural beauty of the *Agave* family also bears closer inspection. The fleshy leaves unfold from a central core and are so closely packed that they leave an indentation on the next leaf and create a pattern of mathematical intricacy. *A. americana* has beautiful blue-grey colouring, although the dull green *A. victoriae-reginae* is more reliable indoors.

Some members of the fig (*Ficus*) family make excellent indoor plants and come in different forms. The weeping fig (*Ficus benjamina*) can grow to a great height given the right conditions. It has a dramatic simplicity of form and, given the space, can be used to link the outside with indoors. This is particularly effective if there is a large expanse of glass between the two areas. Another member of the fig family, the creeping fig (*Ficus pumila*) is a small spreading version that will happily grow at the base of its larger relative. They both respond well to generous feeding. Some specimens of fig are grown for their sculptural beauty. *F. carica*, for example, has clean lines and well-defined branches, the shape of which can be maintained by careful clipping and pruning. *F. benjamina* is considered to be one of the most efficient plants for boosting oxygen levels, removing carbon monoxide and formaldehyde from the air.

Bamboos can be grown indoors where there are high light levels, although they will benefit from being outside for some of the time. Their strong vertical canes contrast with the delicacy of their leaves, making them ideal candidates for the architectural category. They have a Zen-like quality, with gently swaying stems and softly rustling leaves, and make a perfect translucent screen for windows or to delineate spaces.

Over recent years, garden centres have been selling strange, hairy logs that, according to the instructions, will produce exotic shoots from the crown if they are planted in potting mix and watered well. These are the magnificent tree ferns, which originate mainly from New Zealand and Australian rainforests. The cut-log variety is usually *Dicksonia antarctica*, which will do well in a cool conservatory (sun room), provided the trunk is watered almost daily for six months until roots have formed at the base and the spectacular fronds appear from the crown. *D. fibrosa* is usually sold already rooted by specialist nurseries.

above The graceful tree fern *Dicksonia fibrosa* needs a large space for its scale and dignified character to be fully appreciated. Because the roots are present under the fibrous mat of its trunk, it needs to be kept moist and the trunk sprayed on a regular basis.
opposite Though a young specimen, this common fig (*Ficus carica*) has the form of an old gnarled tree. The antique terracotta pot also suggests age and the passing of many seasons. The whole display needs nothing but a white wall to show its structure to best advantage.

cacti and succulents

Part of the appeal of cacti and succulents is that they remind us of ourselves: fat ladies dancing or plump babies playing, or, in the case of cacti, old men with beards. Available in all kinds of shapes and sizes, they are great indoor plants, enjoying warm dry conditions and even thriving on neglect. They share a fleshy, mathematical beauty, often with perfect rosettes and a powdery bloom. They look good in textured containers and, with their geometric forms, complement modern interiors perfectly.

A succulent is a plant with plump, fleshy leaves or stems (or both), which enable it to retain water to help it survive in arid conditions. Cacti are a type of succulent, but in all except a few primitive species the leaves have become modified to spines or hairs and the stems have taken over the function of the leaves – being thick, fleshy and with the ability to photosynthesize.

Cacti are an acquired taste, but, with a little care, they will suddenly amaze you with a flower of such exotic beauty and intense colour that it makes the years of non-flowering worth it. Although most cacti have their natural home in warm, semi-desert regions of the Americas, some grow as epiphytes on trees in the forests of tropical South America. Some of these, such as zygocactus, schlumbergera and rhipsalidopsis, have produced hybrids and varieties that are popular flowering houseplants in winter and spring. There are species that creep and cascade, others that have hairy or cylindrical spiny columns, some with flat jointed pads, and others with globular or candelabra shapes. The only drawback is their prickles. Even those that look soft and silky have a way of penetrating your skin and becoming invisible to the naked eye, although intensely irritating, even painful, to the flesh. Repotting is a task akin to bee-keeping in its need for protective clothing. Children are often attracted to the small-scale and rounded shapes of some cluster-forming varieties such as *Mammillaria zeilmanniana* and *Rebutia fibrigii*, so they should be warned to take care.

Cacti have no "leaves", just a moisture-retaining stem covered with prickles, hairs or spines. They can be propagated easily by breaking off the offsets and sitting them in a stony potting mix. Very large cactus specimens are now available and would make an ideal investment if you have a large loft-style space.

above This elegant collection of sedums makes a striking focal point in a shallow, metal tray on a nest of tables. Top-dressed with a mulch of broken shells, it suggests a hot, dry desert habitat.
opposite Three *Kalanchoe thyrsiflora* stand like ornamental architectural details on a sunny shelf. Very simple terracotta pots echo the texture of the leaves and suit the rosette-like forms.
below left and right *Rebutia fibrigii* and *Mammillaria zeilmanniana* are appealing cacti. They are happy in very little soil, and the new "babies" can be plucked off and propagated quite easily.

One of the most sculptural of cacti is the prickly pear (*Opuntia ficus-indica*), with its amusing, circus-balancing act of flat, prickly discs. The bristles can irritate the skin and are then difficult to remove. The new discs can be removed and propagated into a new plant once they have reached a reasonable size.

Of the other succulents, members of the *Kalanchoe* family make good houseplants. *K. thyrsiflora* has powdery grey-green petals, which are tinged with red at the edges. It will grow unwatered for weeks and still look like some exotic flower, blushing and blooming away quite happily. Kalanchoes look excellent arranged in groups and are a reminder of warm climates even in the middle of a cold winter.

One of the most beautiful succulents for colour and form is the grey-pink *Echeveria* 'Perle von Nürnberg'. Originating from desert areas, it looks absolutely wonderful in a minimal interior where the emphasis is on space and light. Another member of the same family is the sublime silver-grey *Dudleya pulverulenta*, also rosette-shaped, which looks sophisticated in a metallic container, especially if this is top-dressed with coarse white grit.

above By grouping all these objects together, a story is told. The baked clay pot, the gravel and the sun-parched wood all suggest heat and the natural habitat of the well-loved prickly pear cactus (*Opuntia ficus-indica*), which originates from central Mexico. Bowl-shaped, yellow flowers may appear on mature plants in late spring and summer.

left A sense of place is created by siting these very sculptural cacti in front of an old Moroccan door panel, and the composition looks just right.

opposite A simple, but elegant, stone pot is the perfect shape for displaying the strong form and beautiful bronze colouring of these *Echeveria* succulents on an old kitchen table.

a dry garden

For a contemporary space create a sculptural desert garden of agaves and cacti. The advantage of these plants is that they do not require constant watering or attention. In fact, a little neglect will do no harm while you are away on holiday for two weeks.

1 Cover the bottom of the container with a layer of stones, broken pieces of terracotta pot or pieces of polystyrene, to a depth of about 8cm (3in).

2 Fill the container to a depth of about three-quarters with the cactus potting mix and arrange the plants carefully in position. Wear gloves when doing this because the spines will be very sharp. Fill in the gaps with more potting mix, packing in the mix carefully to avoid creating air pockets.

3 Water the plants in well, using tepid water that has stood at room temperature for some time.

4 Cover the surface of the potting mix with a generous top-dressing of grey stone chippings. Not only will this show off the architectural form of the plants, but it will also suggest their natural environment.

you will need

a boldly shaped container

1 large bag of stones, broken terracotta
   pot or pieces of polystyrene
   for drainage

cactus potting mix

1 *Agave americana* 'Marginata'

1 *Agave stricta*

2 *Agave victoriae-reginae*

1 *Pachypodium lamerei*

a pair of gardening gloves

a watering can

grey stone chippings

a minimal garden

Create a contemplative garden of moss and gravel, using primeval-looking living stones (*Lithops*) as rocky outcrops. The simple black-lacquer tray provides a graphic outline to the display. The moss will last a few months, but the living stones will probably outlast you.

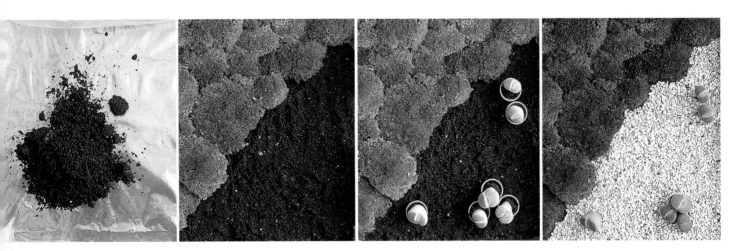

1 Cut a liner of heavy-duty plastic sheeting to fit exactly into the container. Line the container with the sheeting, and cover with cactus potting mix.

2 Arrange the bun moss over half the area, using the best pieces to create little hills. Use the smaller pieces to fill in all the gaps around the edges.

3 Arrange the living stones in their tiny pots, moving them around until they look like ancient rocks in a Japanese monastery, then plant them in the potting mix.

4 Cover all the potting mix with a generous layer of the fine grit and mist the whole arrangement with a fine spray of filtered water or rainwater.

you will need

a sheet of heavy-duty plastic sheeting

a pair of scissors

a shallow container such as a black-
   lacquer tray

cactus potting mix

1 basket of bun moss from a
   florist's shop

6 living stones (*Lithops*)

fine grit sold specifically for cactus displays

spray-mister

colour

We describe our lives as colourful or colourless; we have a language that uses colour to describe emotions, evoke memories, stimulate or calm, and a natural world around us awash with wonderful hues and tints.

bold and brilliant

We all have preferences when it comes to the colours we use in the design of our interiors. The colours of our own indoor plants, as well as those of the walls, floors and soft furnishings, can also be used as an expression of own unique personal style.

Most people use colours from the paler end of the spectrum to paint their homes because light reflects off pale colours and makes walls visually recede, thus giving a feeling of spaciousness. In contrast, darker colours advance, making the room seem smaller and more intimate. However, dark colours are useful in certain situations. Not only do they disguise blemishes, but they also make pictures and objects seen against them stand out more clearly. This is advisable for older or larger houses with high ceilings and less than perfect walls.

In the same way, the use of boldly colourful plants can transform a room and create a powerful focal point. A tiny splash of intense colour can lift a room from being rather ordinary to something highly creative. Think of purple irises in a yellow room, bright orange marigolds or sunflowers in a pale grey one, or the shocking pink, paddle-shaped bracts of *Tillandsia cyanea* wittily teamed with toning towels in an all-white bathroom.

One of the most spectacular, and unusually coloured, plants is *Aeonium* 'Zwartkop', a succulent with fleshy, dark reddish-black rosettes held on branches off a main stem. It likes to be kept cool in winter and needs bright light in spring and summer when its leaves will darken with the light. Not many plants are black, so this is a wonderful piece of plant sculpture for a contemporary setting.

opposite Very few plants are as near black as the architectural succulent *Aeonium* 'Zwartkop'. The contrast between the white pot and the dark rosette-like foliage is bold and striking. The richly coloured leaves look stunning in this contemporary setting.

top right *Tillandsia cyanea* have pink, paddle-shaped bracts with purple-blue flowers along the edge in summer.
right These striking, bright yellow *Narcissus* 'Tête-à-Tête' boldly announce the arrival of spring.

Certain flower colours are seasonal: yellow and blue in spring, pinks, reds and oranges in summer, and more muted oranges and golds in autumn. With plants being flown in from all over the world, this is not a hard-and-fast rule to follow, but it is rewarding to acknowledge the seasons and work with them. Indeed, one of the great joys of spring is to see new green shoots emerging from bulbs and the promise of sunshine in a trough of yellow daffodils. The ritual of planting the dry-looking bulbs in autumn and keeping them in a cool dark place until they have sprouted is supremely satisfying and remarkably easy to achieve. Given enough space you could even create a mini-garden indoors using a group of containers, each filled with a single species to suggest a small landscape. This could vary from season to season, and might not last more than a few weeks, but think of the pleasure of seeing the intense yellow of a buttercup meadow, for example, in a city apartment.

Plants with bright summer colours, such as bougainvilleas and mandevilleas, are best grown in a conservatory (sun room) where they can get the light they need. If you do not have a conservatory, there are other brightly flowered plants that can be grown indoors, such as hybrids of *Kalanchoe blossfeldiana*. These have small, leathery, serrated leaves that often turn reddish in strong sunlight. They have clusters of long-lasting, short-stalked small flowers in shades of red, orange, yellow and lilac. Although naturally spring-flowering plants, commercial growers are able to produce flowering specimens throughout the year.

Ornamental peppers (*Capsicum annuum* Longum Group) can be relied on to make bright, shiny splashes of colour in the autumn, ranging from lipstick-red to polished aubergine to green. Their compact bushiness makes them suitable as a centrepiece on a dining or kitchen table in very simple containers. They are raw and earthy, rather like baked earth, a reminder of hot summers and spicy food, although the ornamental varieties are not edible.

opposite A neatly arranged row of ornamental hot chilli peppers (*Capsicum annuum* Longum Group) make for a bold display on a mantelshelf. The flame-shaped fruits above a fireplace suggest an alternative source of heat to the fire.

pale and pure

The softer pale colours are relaxing, subtle and unthreatening. They can be used in a bedroom to create a soothing atmosphere or in an informal living room or dining area where you can rest, unwind and recuperate from the stresses of the day.

opposite A collection of china, lovingly collected and unified by the simplicity of form of each piece, provides a fitting backdrop for bowls of fragrant lavender.
below The severe black containers prevent this extravagant grid of pink miniature roses looking overly feminine.

For those who find the brilliant white of many modern paints too cold or bland, there are hundreds of whites with the merest hint of pale colour that give a more relaxed feel to walls. Try putting a brighter flower in the same hue against these to bring out the subtlety of colour – it may be all you need to bring the colour alive. Pale walls will also emphasize the shape of the plants, throwing them into stark relief, as well as reflecting light around them.

Pale colours remind us of faded fabrics. The traditional *toile de Jouy* looks so much better when it is a little faded, while denim becomes more interesting after each wash. Linens bleach out in the same way, leaving only a hint of their original colour as a pale distant memory, while part of the essence of the traditional English interior is its well-worn, faded charm.

Subtle colours are also associated with fragility and delicacy. The palest pink cyclamen look utterly vulnerable on their fine stalks, while the soft baby-blue flowers of the climbing Cape leadwort (*Plumbago auriculata*) hang delicately in clusters, making a cool splash in a conservatory (sun room). A pale pink *Phalaenopsis* orchid is a confection of sugary loveliness.

Pale colours can either look pure and innocent or chic and sophisticated. Place pink roses against black and the result is urban chic, a

combination favoured by Coco Chanel, but place them against a billowing, white, muslin curtain, and the look is feminine and natural. Miniature hybrid roses suitable for growing indoors come in a range of colours. Available as bushes or trained as miniature standards, most are derived from *Rosa chinensis* 'Minima', but they will probably be labelled simply as "miniature roses".

Lavender (*Lavandula*) has the attributes of beautiful colouring as well as a heady, sleep-inducing fragrance. Indeed, the wonderful colour of the purple-mauve flowerheads is set off perfectly by the silvery grey foliage and stems. This beautiful plant recalls romantic cottage gardens and purple Provençal fields. Lavender is really a garden plant, but it is simply irresistible for a short time in a bright sunny position indoors on, perhaps, a country dresser.

Pale blue and pure white is another great colour combination, suggesting summer holidays, blue skies and fluffy white clouds. Choose a container in a contrasting colour to the plant – perhaps a white pot for a mauve campanula – but one still in tune with the theme, and then add an appropriate top-dressing. Shells or even tiny starfish would evoke the seaside. Pieces of pale, bleached wood added to a bowl of orchids would create a miniature version of their natural tropical rainforest habitat.

The olive tree (*Olea europaea*), with its delicate tones of pale grey-green and silver, is endowed with an ageless quality, reminding us of ancient Mediterranean hillsides. Although best grown in a conservatory (sun room), it can be kept in a sunny window, and will lend elegance and timelessness to both modern and traditional interiors. For a contemporary design scheme, try planting an olive tree in a zinc or galvanized container to reflect the silvery underside of the leaves. A more traditional setting would call for an antique terracotta or stone container.

above and opposite The silvery grey-green leaves of this olive tree (*Olea europaea*) tone exquisitely with the paintwork of the conservatory. The soft metallic sheen of the seating creates a perfect transition between the house and garden.

whites and creams

Fresh and crisp in spring, cool and refreshing in summer, and ethereal and mystical in winter, whites and creams provide year-round promise. White and cream flowers look wonderful in any style of room, and need only the simplest of containers to show them at their loveliest.

above The dark green leaves of this lacecap hydrangea look stunning against a diaphanous muslin curtain. The contrast between the delicacy of the curtain and the strength of the leaves is marked.
right This exotic *Phalaenopsis* orchid is made even more desirable by its pure white waxiness.
opposite The purity and simplicity of white hyacinths (*Hyacinthus orientalis*) perfectly complement the minimal design of an all-white bedroom.

Glass, white ceramic, steel and Perspex containers, with their clean lines and bold shapes, are perfect for teaming with the simple beauty and delicacy of white and cream flowers. White moth orchids (*Phalaenopsis*) have been somewhat overused in contemporary interiors, but they are still very difficult to beat in terms of sheer elegance of form. The gently drooping stem of gleaming, pure white flowers will last for months and, with a little feeding and the right environment, the orchid should flower again the following year. Considering how exotic these orchids look, they are remarkably good houseplants, despite their initial cost.

The intricate flowers of hydrangeas have a pleasing mathematical order to them and can be used to make bold design statements. The lacecap hydrangea shown here, *Hydrangea macrophylla* 'Veitchii', has large heavily indented leaves and large white flowerheads. Hydrangeas have a rather formal air, which makes them a suitable plant, on a temporary basis, for a more traditional living room or entrance hall. In this setting, the plant would look stunning displayed in an old-fashioned brass or wicker planter or an elegant stone urn. The *hydra* part of the name means "water" so they obviously need plenty of watering. Once they have finished flowering, they can be planted out in the garden where they will eventually become a large shrub.

shades of green

Green promises new hope: green grass after a drought, new leaf buds on bare branches after winter, and green shoots through the soil after a period of cold. In general, plants that lose their green colouring are in poor health, lacking minerals, light or water.

We bring greenery into our homes to remind us of the organic world and of what is precious in our environment. Green is not just one colour, but a riot of different shades, ranging from the pale silvery grey greens of olives and agaves to the darkest holly greens, with all kinds of golden greens and lime greens in between. There are few things more beautiful than light illuminating the structure of leaves. Try looking through the leaves of the African hemp (*Sparrmannia africana*) for a really chlorophyll-rich, oxygenating experience. The complexity of leaf forms is also more clearly seen in green. The delicate leaves of the club rush (*Isolepsis cernua*), for example, are light, airy and thin, giving the plant an ethereal presence.

The pineapple lily (*Eucomis autumnalis*), a bulb that flowers outdoors in late summer and autumn, can be brought inside to great effect. The leaves are glossy and strap-like, but the extraordinary flowerhead is the star of the show. It is much better seen at close quarters – the pineapple-shaped head of tiny and beautifully marked flowers clustering tightly around a spotted stem is topped off with a slightly comic hairdo of small leaflets. Allow the potting mix to gradually dry out after the flowerhead has wilted and keep the bulbs in a cool, dry place ready for replanting in early spring.

top left The legs of the pots and the hair-like club rush (*Isolepsis cernua*) make a humorous partnership. The foliage of this grass is a beautiful fresh shade of green.
centre left The spiky, sculptural leaves of the succulent *Agave americana* are a beautiful blue-green.

bottom left Trailing ivy (*Hedera helix*) is happy to grow in low light levels and a moist atmosphere, and exhibits a wide range of green, yellow and cream tones in its variegated forms.
opposite The flowerhead of the pineapple lily (*Eucomis autumnalis*) is composed of numerous tiny, creamy green flowers.

a lime-green garden

Green is a refreshing and invigorating colour. The leaves of these insect-eating plants need to be seen at close quarters if you are to fully appreciate the complexity of the shading. Placed in a conservatory (sun room), they will also help to control flying pests organically.

1 If you intend to make this a permanent display, ensure the bowl has drainage holes. Half fill the bowl with potting mix, remembering to add a layer of drainage material in the bottom first.

2 Taking the plants from their plastic pots, arrange the tall pitcher plants in the centre and add more potting mix to within 2cm (1in) of the rim of the bowl.

3 Arrange the Venus flytraps around the edge of the bowl, spacing them out evenly. Gently firm in the potting mix with your fingers.

4 Water in the plants well, using rainwater or boiled water that has been allowed to cool down. Tap water is unsuitable for these plants.

you will need

a large bowl, measuring approximately
   50cm (20in) in diameter
drainage material, such as stones, gravel,
   broken pieces of old terracotta pot or
   pieces of polystyrene
potting mix made up of two-thirds
   peat substitute and one-third perlite or
   washed sand
3 pitcher plants (*Sarracenia*)
7 Venus flytraps (*Dionaea muscipula*)
small indoor gardening tools or an old
   long-handled kitchen spoon
rainwater or cooled boiled water

a scented white garden

This gloriously scented arrangement of pure white flowers combined with the rich green, textural foliage will last far longer than a vase of cut flowers. The plants are simply placed in the decorative display container in their individual pots, and can be replaced at any time.

1 Loosely line the container with the plastic sheeting in order to prevent water from damaging the container or furniture.

2 Plunge the pots in a bucket of water and drain before arranging. Place the gardenias in their pots around the edge of the container, leaving room between each one for a potted rose.

3 Arrange the potted roses alternately between the gardenias.

4 Fill the central void with the jasmine and, if need be, add some moss between the plants to hide any gaps.

you will need

a large interesting container, in this case
   an antique leather water carrier
a sheet of heavy-duty plastic sheeting
a bucket of water
white gardenias (*Gardenia augusta*
   'Veitchiana'), white miniature roses (*Rosa*)
   and white jasmine (*Jasminum*
   polyanthum) in equal quantities
moss, if necessary

seasonal displays

It is immensely satisfying to follow the rhythm of the seasons when gardening indoors. Reflecting seasonal changes gives our creative plant arrangements an added poignancy and helps keep us in touch with nature.

spring

Indoor bulbs can be a wonderful antidote to short days in spring when it is too chilly outdoors. The miracle of beauty emerging from an unprepossessing bulb is always a delight.

Each autumn, you can have great fun visiting a specialist bulb supplier, and, armed with a collection of brown paper bags, filling them with bulbs in a variety of sizes and with wondrously complex shapes. Some have papery skins, tinged with purple, others are textured like rhinoceros hide, but all have a mane of little roots. Choose firm, healthy ones, and just add water. Most spring flowers like to be cool, so they are ideal for growing in hallways. Don't forget to buy summer- and autumn-flowering bulbs, such as Oriental lilies and pineapple lily (*Eucomis autumnalis*), in early spring.

The resulting plants lend themselves to both traditional and modern interiors, depending on the container you choose. Let the flowers do the showing off and choose a container that blends seamlessly with the style of your interior. Bulbs do not need soil in the short term for nourishment, merely to stabilize them. By using glass or Perspex containers, almost filled with gravel or stones, you can watch the roots grow and easily judge the amount of water the plant needs. The bulb should be suspended above, but not touching, the water to prevent rotting.

Usually the first flowers to break through the winter soil are the crocuses with their pretty, little, vase-shaped flowers in yellow, white or purple. A large bowl of these tiny innocents would evoke a small garden,

above left A striking mass of early purple *Crocus vernus* looks smart in a round Perspex container.
centre left A row of sprouting daffodil and iris bulbs are planted in alternately coloured pots for an understated study in green, white and silver.

bottom left *Iris* 'George' is a Reticulata iris with beautiful markings. Planted in a row, it is easy to admire the delicate flowers.
opposite *Cyclamen coum* have elegant, nodding flowers in a range of colours, including pinks, reds, purples, salmon and white. They are available in different sizes.

although they do not last for long in a warm environment. Plant the old bulbs outside after flowering. The intense deep purple of *Iris* 'George', with little else but its complex flowerhead showing above the planting medium, is strangely beautiful. Set the purple off against blue-grey slate chippings for maximum impact and use a silver or glass container. A geometric yellow pot would also be dramatic and make a bold statement.

The pure white flowers of heavily perfumed hyacinths (*Hyacinthus orientalis*) are perhaps the epitome of spring. They would create a strong sculptural effect in a fireplace in a modern apartment, top-dressed with white pebbles and with a layer of moss to hide the potting mix.

In contrast, the ethereal beauty of paper-white *Narcissus papyraceus* will work well in any style of home. The flowers also have the loveliest of scents. The stems often need supporting as they reach up to the light. Use bare branches and twigs, as these look much more natural than bought canes and create a sense of the outdoors. Simple baskets with heavy-duty plastic stapled around the top inner edge make a more traditional container and an attractive present topped with a dressing of moss.

above and top These fragrant white hyacinths (*Hyacinthus orientalis*) have been planted in a Perspex trough and top-dressed with white pebbles.
opposite A simple basket is just the right container for these beautifully scented, paper-white narcissi (*Narcissus papyraceus*). The addition of woodland twigs is both functional and decorative.

summer

Summer is a time for flowers in the brightest colours and headiest scents, as well as of ripening fruits. It is also when hot sunshine shining through glass can damage plants, scorching the leaves and drying out the potting mix, so constant vigilance is important.

above Float water hyacinths (*Eichhornia crassipes*) in a large bowl of water for the ultimate in chic. With summery cut flowers either arranged or floating in other glass bowls nearby, it makes a strong seasonal statement.
opposite and right These dark red pelargoniums are literally sunbathing in their metal containers.

Although perfect for ripening luscious purple aubergines (eggplant) and fiery red tomatoes on kitchen windowsills, summer is really the time to be outside in the garden. If you don't have a garden, bring the outside indoors and use plants, such as bowls of miniature strawberries, to remind you of outdoor celebrations and lazy picnics. For a natural, informal feel, plant a mass of colourful nasturtiums, which are easy to grow from seed, in a galvanized trough. Their pretty round leaves, some with variegations, set off the multicoloured flowers beautifully. The flowers are edible and make simple salads look pretty and summery.

Watery delights are very much a part of summer too. For an unusual, cooling display, float aquatic plants in a large glass bowl or tank. They do not need any soil, getting all their nutrients from the water. Water hyacinths (*Eichhornia crassipes*) have bulbous stems, rounded leaves and a delicate, but short-lived, flower, rather like a faded blue hyacinth. Water lettuce (*Pistia stratiotes*) has strongly ribbed leaves and would look starkly modern as a table decoration, the hair-like roots fanning out beneath the greenery for added interest. For an even more minimal display, float the leaves of the moss-like *Azolla filiculoides* in bowls of water beside each place setting. They look stunning with garden tags, with the guests' names written in waterproof green ink, floating in the water. Use bottled water or rainwater because hard tap water will make the leaves go brown and the plants will eventually die.

Some plants are so beautiful in every way that they take your breath away. The bird-of-paradise (*Strelitzia reginae*) is one such plant. It has blue-grey, lance-shaped leaves held high on rigid stems in a sculptural clump. The leaves are majestic, but the flowers are the most spectacular show of exotic, bird-like forms, with vibrant spathes and purple and orange flowers resembling a cabaret of plumed dancers. The flowers are sequential: when one plume dies down, another pops up so that the show goes on. If the replacement fails to pop out of the spathe, just hook your finger inside the green "beak" and help the new flower to emerge. They only flower when the plant has reached maturity at about six years old and do best in a conservatory (sun room) or a room with large areas of glazing.

Less demanding and equally beautiful is the arum or calla lily, *Zantedeschia*

above The superb bird-of-paradise (*Strelitzia reginae*) needs warmth and light, so it is perfect for a penthouse or conservatory. Its spiky form is best seen silhouetted against white walls.
opposite The sheer indulgence and luxury of white sofas, a white rug and huge pots of white arum lilies (*Zantedeschia aethiopica*) is seen here to great effect.

aethiopica. The classic variety has pure white spathes, furled and elegant, but there are now many hybrids available in other colours, such as dark red or flecked with golden yellow. The leaves are sometimes spotted with translucent white flecks and are beautiful in their own right. Put a group of plants in a large container to create the massed effect of their natural habitat. *Spathiphyllum wallisii* is grown for its arum-lily-like, white flowers and thin, lance-shaped leaves. Other species and hybrids are available, but *S. wallisii* is compact and one of the most popular. It is very elegant and would look serenely beautiful planted in a white ceramic container, although it may need protection from the hottest summer sun.

autumn

This is the time when fruits and berries have ripened, the light is more golden and diffuse, and colours are more muted and neutral. Most gardens are past their best in the autumn and having some fresh greenery indoors is an added seasonal bonus.

above The strangely beautiful carnivorous tropical pitcher plant, *Nepenthes* 'Director G.T. Moore', with its unusual "pitchers", creates an interesting still-life with a row of elegant white vases.
opposite These spiky succulents, *Aloe ferox*, have rust-coloured tips and suit their metallic zinc planters perfectly. Arranged in a neat row down the centre of a black slate table, they make for a strong sculptural statement.

Many flowering plants bought or grown in the summer will continue to flower well into the autumn if they are watered and fed properly. African violets (*Saintpaulia*), geraniums (*Pelargonium*) and *Streptocarpus* will all produce flowers until mid-autumn and beyond. If you have a balcony or patio, many outdoor bulbs can be grown in pots and then brought indoors when they are about to flower. The plants should be acclimatized first, raising the temperature gradually before bringing them into a warm room. Late summer and autumn bulbs, such as some varieties of lily (*Lilium*) and the pineapple plant (*Eucomis autumnalis*), with its extraordinarily complex flowerhead, make for an unusual display, while the autumn crocus (*Colchicum autumnale*) is sold in mid- and late summer for autumn flowering.

If you have green fingers, try growing some carnivorous plants. The most exotic of these is the tropical pitcher plant, *Nepenthes* 'Director G.T. Moore', whose deep pitchers grow from the extended mid-rib of the leaf. In the wild, the pitcher rim secretes nectar that attracts insects who then fall in. The only problem is that pitcher plants need high temperatures and equally high humidity to keep going, but they are a truly organic way of dealing with unwanted pests.

Succulents make good year-round plants, so they are ideal for the autumn. Their soft, often silvery, colouring also gives them a suitable mellowness at this time of year. The elegant *Aloe ferox*, for example, has

rust-red marginal teeth or spikes that suit the seasonal autumnal colours. Planted in multiple pots and then lined up the length of a dining table, they create an interesting sculptural effect. Their strong succulent leaves make a refreshing change when dead leaves are falling outside and the rest of the garden is shutting down for the winter.

The unusual kangaroo paw plant (*Anigozanthos flavidus*) can flower all year round in a conservatory (sun room), but the velvety flowerheads and the clump-like habit make a comforting arrangement for this time of year. The yellow-green to brownish-red flowers look rather like flickering flames. Planted in a burnished copper bowl and top-dressed with a grey pebble mulch, they would make a warm, cheerful display.

To match this time of plenty, grow ornamental cabbages and kales (*Brassica oleracea*), which come in a range of colours from deep dark purple to the milkiest of creams mixed with green. With their frilled leaves and rosette-like form, they resemble intricate fabrics. The only disadvantage is that, being small brassicas, they begin to smell unpleasant with time. The ornamental varieties are not edible, so just enjoy them for their vibrant colouring and frilly ostentation. They produce their best colours as the temperature drops in autumn and winter. They flourish best in the cold outdoors, so only bring them in for a short time. Planted in shallow, white or black bowls, they have a Zen-like stillness.

opposite and above right The kangaroo paw plant (*Anigozanthos flavidus*), with its rich colouring and fascinatingly hairy flowers, makes an unusual display in a fireplace before the winter fires are lit.
right Ornamental cabbages (*Brassica oleracea*) have frilly, variegated leaves. The autumnal colouring is ideal in a cool hallway.

winter

When the garden is largely dormant, indoor plants can bring colour to our homes. Centrally heated homes with chilly windowsills, and maybe a draughty hall, are disaster areas for all but the most stoical of plants. This is a time when the truly tried-and-tested, evergreen houseplants come into their own.

Some houseplants, such as the ubiquitous spider plant and rubber plant, are creeping back into fashion as ironic statements, reminders that too much good taste can be lacking in humour. In the past, these survivors stayed in their shiny brown pots, proud to be seen in plastic. They can be shown in a new light, however, especially if they are planted in a contemporary pot that is in keeping with current design trends.

There are, however, other suitable foliage plants with sculptural qualities that perfectly complement modern furniture and current styles of architecture. The velvety green leaves of the Kris plant (*Alocasia sanderiana*) are balanced on the end of long, thin stems. The waxy, dark green, pointed leaves also have remarkable white veining. This plant needs to be grown in hot and humid, tropical conditions, but it is well worth a try, and is perfect for growing in a conservatory (sun room). If you do not have a conservatory, the splendid giant taro (*Alocasia macrorrhiza*) is an excellent alternative. The huge leaves are easily damaged, so make sure you give this plant plenty of space to appreciate its magnificent beauty. Remember its origins in swampy areas of South-east Asia, and keep it well watered and misted.

To have a tree growing indoors seems to be the ultimate triumph, a reversal of what is expected and a validation of your gardening abilities. *Ficus* 'Ali King', a large specimen of the fig family, has a mass of long, dark green, glossy leaves and elegant, pendulous branches. It could be the only plant you need to refresh your spirits during a grey winter.

above Plant and ornaments marry well here, with the rounded bowls echoing the pleasing rounded shape of this hybrid *Begonia* 'Norah Bedson'. With leaves as delightful as these, who needs flowers?
opposite The huge leaves of the giant taro (*Alocasia macrorrhiza*) can reach 30–40cm (12–16in) in length, so this dramatic evergreen plant will create a magnificent focal point in a living room.

There are also a large number of begonias available with gaudy colours and markings that are all easy to grow, propagate and give to friends. One, however, stands out from all the rest. It is a *Begonia* hybrid, which is usually referred to as 'Tiger', although it is more like a green moth in its quivering delicacy than a tiger. A pleasing little plant, with slightly pink fleshy stems and rounded leaves that are strongly marked with pale spots and dark veins, it loves to be cool and a little damp. Plunge the whole pot into water and remove rather than over-water.

Early winter sees a plethora of seasonal pot plants, including the red poinsettia (*Euphorbia pulcherrima*). The green-and-white versions are easier to fit into a modern setting. There is a wealth of other brightly coloured plants that are available all through winter, including *Jasminum polyanthum*, azalea (*Rhododendron simsii*) and *Cyclamen persicum*. Hybrids of *C. persicum* are available in every shade of pink, red, white and purple, as well as bicolour combinations. Think of pure white cyclamen in a galvanized metal window box, underplanted with ivy (*Hedera helix*) for a chic display. For an unlimited colour choice, consider growing *Primula obconica*, which can have flowers in white, blue and apricot, as well as various shades of pink, crimson and scarlet. It is known commonly as the poison primrose because its leaves can cause dermatitis if handled by anyone allergic to it.

Hippeastrum, which is often commonly referred to as amaryllis, is a large flowering bulb for winter. The power of the huge shoot appearing out of a large brown bulb and opening into a graceful, elegant flower is truly wonderful. They happily grow without soil, as long as the bulb is suspended above water. The white roots weave their way though whatever medium you choose: stones, gravel or glass marbles.

above A fine specimen tree in a clutter-free interior should be regarded as an investment piece. This fig, *Ficus* 'Ali King', will grow happily in the window for years. The planting basket has been top-dressed with a mulch of moss, but no other decoration is needed.

right Winter hellebores have to be cold in order to do well, so they will flourish if you live in a freezing Scottish castle, otherwise they are really only suitable for a fleeting visit indoors.

opposite Clipped box standards (*Buxus*) bring a touch of greenery indoors during a cold winter. They are really garden plants, but will be fine if they are brought indoors for just a few days, perhaps for a special occasion.

a summer meadow

Bring the pleasures of a wild-flower meadow into an urban setting with this display of wheat grass and buttercup-yellow tickseed. Health-food stores sell wheat grass or a growing kit – keep clipping the grass and add to the juicer for a healthy drink.

1 Cover the bottom of each container with a layer of drainage material. You will need to plant up two containers with wheat grass and two with tickseed.

2 Add a layer of potting mix to the first container, and, with a sharp knife, cut the wheat grass to fit the container precisely. Repeat for the other container of wheat grass.

3 Remove the tickseed plants from their plastic pots and pack tightly into the two remaining containers. Add more potting mix to fill in any gaps.

4 Water in all the plants well. This is not a long-lasting display, but then neither are some summers.

you will need

4 square metal containers or a large tray

drainage material, such as stones,
    gravel, broken pieces of old terracotta
    pot or pieces of polystyrene

a large tray of sprouted wheat grass
    (*Elymus*)

2 trays of tickseed (*Coreopsis*)

a small bag of loam-based potting mix

a sharp carving knife

a watering can

a winter garden

Winter beauty can be transparent and icy, stark and silvery, a time when forms are seen more clearly and textures have an eerie, frozen quality. A linear arrangement of found objects and plants celebrates this still silence before the start of spring.

1 Fill one of the compartments of the container with the glass pebbles or clear marbles.

2 In another compartment, plant the *Echeveria* 'Perle von Nürnberg' in its pot, if possible, and mulch with the metaleis.

3 Stand the tree-like twigs in the next compartment, using the Spanish moss to provide anchorage.

4 Use the winter seed-heads or cut or dried flowers to add texture to the last compartment, packing them tightly together.

you will need

a long, narrow chrome or steel container, with different compartments

glass pebbles or clear marbles

1 *Echeveria* 'Perle von Nürnberg' or any succulent with silver leaves

metaleis (this is a metal-coated gravel used in aquaria)

dried tree-like twigs or dried flowerheads in interesting shapes

Spanish moss (a grey, stringy moss-like plant available from florist's shops)

round seed-heads or cut or dried flowers

edible plants

The immediacy of watching seeds grow in front of your eyes into an edible crop is intensely satisfying and a delight for all the senses. To have achieved this on a sunny window ledge is doubly special.

salad leaves and herbs

Most foods taste better when only a few minutes have elapsed between harvesting and eating. Leaves are crisper and retain their nutritional value if they are cut just before eating, while vegetables often have a wonderful smell that is totally lost by the time they reach the supermarket.

Most of us have a sunny windowsill where we can start off a few seeds and watch them sprout, or plant some seedlings from a nursery. It is also rewarding to encourage children to grow things that they can eat, such as mustard and cress seeds, which can be sown on layers of wet kitchen paper. They can watch the plants germinate and uncurl, wearing their seeds on their heads like little hats. Growing salads indoors ensures that slugs and snails don't taste them before you do. Seed suppliers sell packets of mixed leaves for using in salads. These can be sown throughout the growing season on a windowsill, sowing more seeds when one crop has been exhausted. Not only do they taste delicious, but they look wonderful with their different colours and textures. Snip the young leaves before they become too large, and the plant will go on producing more leaves. Keep the plants cool and moist to prevent them running to seed.

One of the easiest and most decorative salad plants to grow is ruby or rhubarb chard (*Beta vulgaris*), with its glorious red stems and green leaves, deeply veined with bright scarlet. Push a few of the seeds into a small

top left The immediacy of having juicy young salad leaves growing on your kitchen windowsill is utterly irresistible – and they look glorious, too.
left Mustard and cress in night-light holders make a delightfully simple table decoration. Children will love them.

opposite This is an aphid's-eye view of light streaming through the beautifully marked leaves of these seedlings of ruby or rhubarb chard (*Beta vulgaris*). Snipped into salads, they not only add colour and zest, but the vitamins will be retained if they are eaten immediately.

container of potting mix, and, within a week, fresh young leaves will appear. These are best eaten small and sweet. If the plants are allowed to grow, they will start to resemble spinach and lose their windowsill appeal. Grow them just to see the light shining through the beautiful leaves.

Herbs make rewarding additions to the kitchen windowsill, and, while the pot-grown ones from supermarkets may last for a week or so, they have been unnaturally forced and seem to have a built-in auto-destruct date. It is much better to buy young plants from a garden centre or farmers' market. Try to choose a variety of different herbs. Basil, coriander (cilantro), oregano, chives, marjoram, parsley and mint can all be grown indoors. They all seem to thrive when given the odd dose of diluted liquid tomato feed and plenty of light. Windowsills can get very hot during the summer, however, so check regularly that the potting mix does not dry out completely. Herbs do not overwinter well indoors because of the low light levels, so it is better to start again with new plants in spring. They can easily be grown from seed each year, but it is even easier to buy new plants from the garden centre.

Admittedly, herbs do not always make the most beautiful houseplants, but they have the added bonus of smelling wonderful, particularly when they are brushed against, and fill a kitchen with an aroma that suggests imaginative and innovative food. To have taste, smell and medicinal uses

above and opposite, bottom A mini-potager in an old trug makes a visual as well as a gastronomic feast. The pungent thyme, *Thymus* 'Hartington Silver', creates a lush mat. It is backed by purple basil (*Ocimum basilicum* 'Purple Ruffles'), Japanese parsley and mint (*Mentha*). Keep snipping back these herbs in order to encourage bushy growth.

opposite, top A simple pot of rosemary (*Rosmarinus officinalis*) makes a fragrant addition to a kitchen dining table, but it would be happier on a sunny window ledge outside for most of the time.

all available at your fingertips on your kitchen windowsill takes some beating. However, it is vitally important that you take advice on using herbs medicinally as they can have strong side effects.

Some of the best organic producers sell collections of mixed herb varieties, such as five different types of basil or Oriental herb mixtures. Choose unusual varieties that the supermarkets do not sell and try them out in recipes. There are also some edible flower collections that include nasturtiums, borage, pot marigold and bergamot. Salads look amazing when strewn with nasturtium flowers and leaves, or marigold petals, while a summer's day would not be complete without a glass of Pimms with a few pretty blue borage flowers floating on top. Another particularly beautiful herb is lemon verbena (*Aloysia triphylla*), an elegant plant with lance-shaped leaves and a very strong lemon smell. You can use the leaves in finger bowls for dinner parties and infused in ice creams and sorbets, or dried as potpourri or in scented sachets for the linen closet.

Scented pelargonium leaves can be used to scent and flavour food, with the leaves being removed before eating. Use varieties such as *Pelargonium graveolens*, *P. odoratissimum*, or *P.* 'Attar of Roses' to flavour sorbets, infusing them in a sugar-and-water mix, like a tisane, and removing the leaves after about fifteen minutes. You can also decorate the top of a sponge cake by arranging individual leaves and then sprinkling with icing (confectioners') sugar. Remove the leaves carefully to reveal the perfect outline of a leaf.

tender fruits

It is possible to grow many fruiting plants indoors, ideally in a conservatory, but you can also grow them with care on a sunny windowsill. The joys of dwarf tomatoes, chilli and bell peppers, and aubergines (eggplant), as well as a wealth of colourful citrus fruits, all await the indoor gardener.

opposite Lemon trees (*Citrus limon*) frame the walkway from a shady living room to a sunny conservatory.
right Feeding and watering are the keys to success with citrus plants such as this orange. Don't forget to watch out for scale insects.
below The fruits of the kumquat (*Fortunella japonica*) look like small oranges. It is an attractive evergreen bush for the conservatory and produces plenty of fruit.

Small citrus trees look spectacular in a conservatory (sun room), or a very sunny living or dining room. Their shape lends itself to quite formal rooms – think of elegant orangeries with stone columns and wooden planters filled with specimen orange and lemon trees. Ideally, the containers should be equipped with carrying handles so that the trees can be easily moved to spend the summer outside and winter inside.

Citrus fruits are not difficult to grow given the right conditions. As with most plants, you need to consider the growing conditions. Think of places where they flourish best: in Florida and California, and the countries around the Mediterranean, where they grow on dry, sunny hillsides. When it rains, they are soaked for a short time, but the water then drains away easily. Create the same conditions for your pot-grown varieties, and never let them get waterlogged. Feed them with sequestered iron occasionally and check for scale insect and whitefly.

Kumquats (*Fortunella japonica*) are attractive small evergreen trees that produce fruits like miniature oranges. The flowers are deliciously scented and the fruits can be frozen whole and used instead of ice cubes in cold drinks. They also look festive if used as a temporary top-dressing under winter hyacinths for a dining-table arrangement, with a few of the shiny

top Kitchen utensils can be used to display plants to great effect. These bell peppers (*Capsicum annuum* Grossum Group) are growing happily in a metal pan. **above** Aubergines (*Solanum melongena*), with their luscious purple fruits, are surprisingly easy and rewarding to grow.

green leaves pushed in between for glorious contrast. Keep the leaves of all citrus plants clean by wiping them occasionally. They should also be given a regular foliar feed during winter.

Dwarf tomatoes are happy indoors if they are given sunlight, tomato food and plenty of water. They will ripen even if they fall off their stems while they are still green. The flavour and smell will remind you of how tomatoes should be, and, if they are grown from organic seed and without the use of pesticides, they are very beneficial to your health. Once fruiting, they will need staking as the bunches of tomatoes become too heavy for what is rather a spindly little plant.

It would be possible, in fact, to grow a complete *ratatouille* of tomatoes, aubergines (eggplant) and sweet (bell) peppers, provided you can give them the sunlight needed to ripen them. Aubergines (*Solanum melongena*) are not perhaps the most beautiful of plants, although they have interesting sharp prickles on the backs of their leathery leaves. A small, white, star-shaped flower produces the shiny fruit. This will also need staking, the parent plant being too small to support its ungainly offspring. Mist the leaves regularly.

Sweet peppers (*Capsicum annuum* Grossum Group) are easy to grow, given high humidity and warmth. Mist the flowers daily and pinch out the growing tips of young plants to encourage them to bush out. Members of the same family, but with a dramatically different taste, are the hot chilli peppers (*C. annuum* Longum Group), which are highly decorative, with their pendent cone-shaped fruit.

Other edible plants to grow indoors include oyster and button (white) mushrooms. These are not as difficult to grow as you might think. Growing methods involve creating warm moist conditions for the oyster mushroom spawn to take on its growing medium, usually some form of recycled wood product, then shocking it into thinking that winter has arrived by putting it into a refrigerator for a week or so. Once the fruiting cycle is established, the little oyster mushrooms will need a cool, light, humid place and will grow into the most beautiful shapes.

This makes a spectacular and original display for a table centrepiece, but be aware that some people are allergic to the mushrooms or the spores produced by them (or to both). Button mushrooms are easier to grow if you have a warm room somewhere large enough for a 15kg (33lb) bag of potting mix. They do not fit so easily into the stylish interior category, but are quite irresistible for the adventurous indoor gardener. Specialist companies will supply all the information needed to grow mushrooms.

Having suggested all the ingredients for a home-grown vegetarian meal, perhaps we should include a few strawberries to finish the meal with something sweet. Alpine strawberries (*Fragaria vesca*) like to trail or creep, and need plenty of bright light. The leaves and flowers are pretty in their own right, and the sweet fruit is an added bonus. Strawberry plants would make a delightful decoration for a summer dining table.

above Alpine strawberries (*Fragaria vesca*) look fresh and summery in identical cream pots. They have a better flavour than many of the cultivated varieties. Water and feed strawberries on a regular basis to ensure a good crop.

a salad leaf garden

There is nothing quite like the tangy taste of crisp young salad leaves, cut and eaten in moments. Keep cutting the leaves in order to encourage further growth. Sprinkle seeds in any planting gaps whenever necessary to maintain fresh crops throughout the summer.

1 Sow the seeds in a clean seed tray, using the seedling potting mix. Water in well and place under a sheet of glass until the seeds have germinated.

2 Prick out the seedlings carefully with the small trowel or fork, taking care not to damage the delicate new roots and leaves.

3 Plant the seedlings in their final positions in the window box, using a loam-based potting mix, adding a layer of drainage material first. Water in well.

4 Snip and eat the salad leaves regularly to encourage further growth, adding more seeds to any bare patches to ensure a continuous supply.

you will need

a clean seed tray

seedling potting mix

a packet of mixed variety salad leaf seeds

a packet of ruby chard (*Beta vulgaris*) seeds

a watering can

a sheet of glass

a small trowel or fork

a large window box or trough

drainage material, such as stones,
    gravel, broken pieces of old terracotta
    pot or pieces of polystyrene

loam-based potting mix

plant labels

a tomato and basil garden

Classic Italian dishes are often based around the sublimely fragrant mix of tomatoes and basil. Using dwarf tomatoes and two different varieties of basil, you can grow your own simple appetizer, which smells and tastes as good as it looks.

1 Place a layer of drainage material in the bottom of the trough and cover with a layer of potting mix.

2 Place the tomato plants in their final planting positions. They should be spaced at 15cm (6in) intervals.

3 Place the purple basil in the gaps between the tomato plants at the front of the trough, and the green basil behind.

4 Firm the plants in with more potting mix and water in well. Feed with a tomato fertilizer on a weekly basis. When ripe, slice the tomatoes, sprinkle with chopped basil, drizzle with extra virgin olive oil and eat.

you will need

drainage material, such as stones, gravel, broken pieces of old terracotta pot or pieces of polystyrene

a long, narrow, wooden trough, approximately 20cm (8in) deep and 15cm (6in) wide

loam-based potting mix

4 dwarf tomato plants (*Lycopersicon esculentum*)

5 purple basil plants (*Ocimum basilicum* 'Purple Ruffles')

3 green basil plants (*Ocimum basilicum*)

a small trowel

a watering can

tomato fertilizer

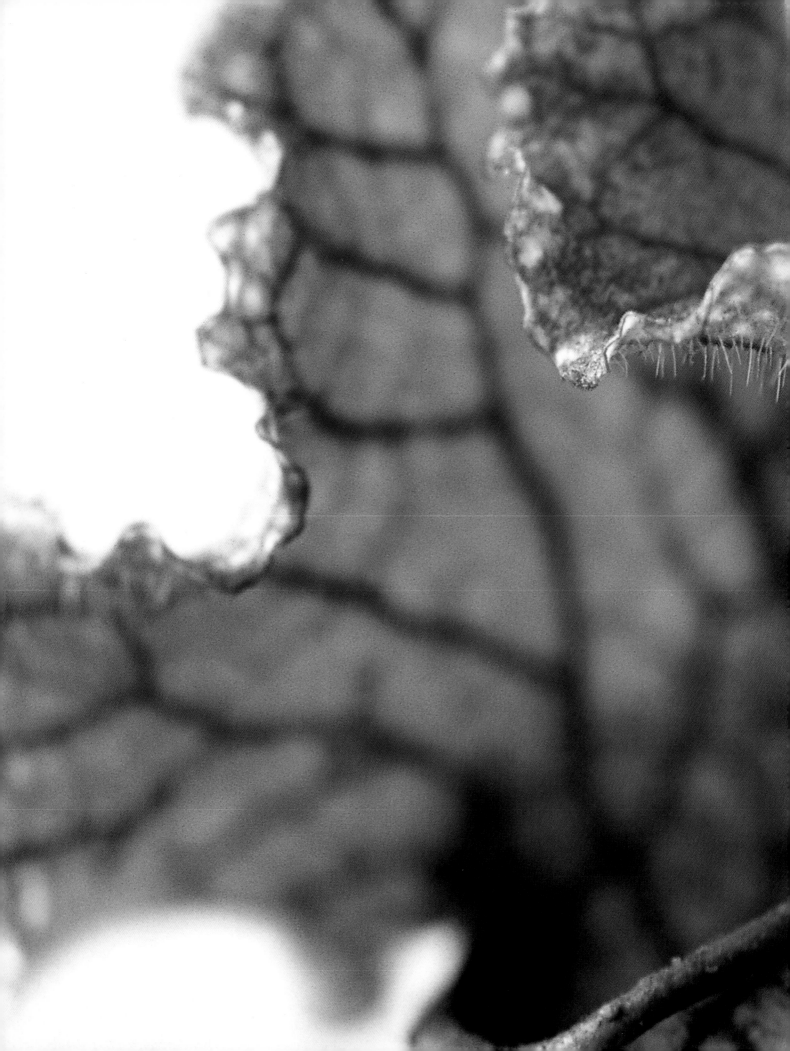

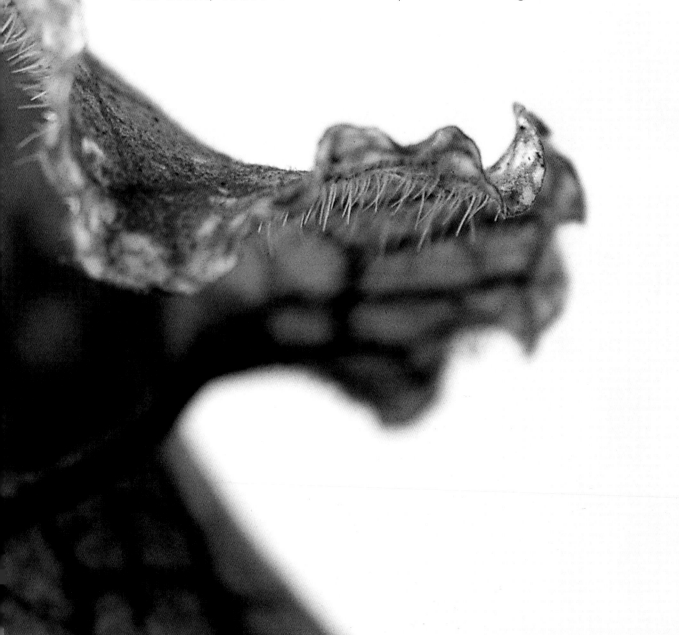

plant focus

Most plants have many interesting attributes and those featured in this section have been arranged into categories – plants for sculpture, colour and scent, seasonal interest and plants for eating.

plants for sculpture

Many plants fall into this category, being valued for their strong form rather than for the beauty or scent of their flowers. Their outline, when seen against a plain white wall, will need no other decoration as their graphic quality stands alone.

Blechnum gibbum

Cyperus involucratus

Dicksonia fibrosa

Ficus carica

Architectural Plants

Blechnum gibbum
Hard fern
This is an evergreen fern with tall, lance-shaped fronds that uncurl beautifully from the centre. It can also be grown successfully in the garden.
Light Bright/indirect.
Temperature Cool.
Watering and feeding Keep moist. Mist regularly or stand in a tray of damp gravel. Apply a high-nitrogen liquid fertilizer at half strength occasionally when in growth.
Cultivation Pot on in spring, using a loam-based potting mix with added bark, charcoal and sharp sand.

Cyperus involucratus
Umbrella plant
This clump-forming plant, which looks like a collection of umbrellas, grows in water in the wild, but it can be grown as a houseplant if it is given enough moisture. Small, yellowish-white flowers appear in summer.
Light Bright/indirect.
Temperature Cool.
Watering and feeding Keep waterlogged at all times. Stand the pot in a shallow tray of water; a piece of charcoal will keep the water "sweet". Apply a balanced liquid fertilizer monthly when in growth.
Cultivation In spring, divide overcrowded plants and pot up in a loam-based potting mix, top-dressed with gravel.

Dicksonia
Tree fern
D. fibrosa is a dramatic fern, with beautiful curls on the new fronds, a good specimen plant for a cool conservatory (sun room). Many of the tree ferns sold at garden centres are *D. antarctica*, which is bought as a log rather than in a pot. The log should be soaked thoroughly first and then put in a pot which is deep enough to stabilize the plant, and no more. Tree ferns are sold by length, so try not to waste an inch. They will grow up to 2.1m (7ft) in the home. There are roots in the fibrous mass of old leaf bases, but it will probably take a year for the cut log to form new roots.

During this time, it is important that the root-containing trunk is kept moist. Some growers recommend watering the crown as well. Tree ferns can also be put outdoors during summer where they bring an exotic atmosphere to a courtyard garden or patio.
Light Bright/filtered.
Temperature Cool/humid.
Watering and feeding Water the trunk so that it is constantly damp and apply a high-nitrogen liquid fertilizer monthly.
Cultivation Pot on when roots appear in the drainage holes of the container, using a loam-based potting mix with added bark, charcoal and leaf mould.

Ficus Fig

The figs used as houseplants are grown for their foliage. The common fig (*F. carica*) can grow up to 2.1m (7ft) in the home, but a younger plant looks spectacular displayed on a plinth. *F.* 'Ali King' is an evergreen that enjoys being indoors. The long, shiny, elliptical leaves are held on slender elegant branches. The weeping fig (*F. benjamina*) can grow to 1.5m (5ft) given the right conditions and is one of the most effective plants for purifying the air. The creeping fig (*F. pumila*) is a delicate, evergreen, trailing climber that looks good growing underneath larger specimens, creating a green carpet of tiny leaves. Figs may lose their leaves if shocked by draughts, lack of water or being moved.

Light Bright/filtered.
Temperature Warm, average room.
Watering and feeding Water freely when in growth (large plants will need frequent watering as the larger area of the leaves loses water faster). Feed monthly with a high-nitrogen liquid fertilizer when in growth. Figs respond well to generous feeding.
Cultivation When pot-bound, pot on using a loam-based mix with added bark.

Musa acuminata 'Dwarf Cavendish'
Banana

The evergreen, paddle-shaped leaves are huge, but damage easily. The plant can grow up to 2.1m (7ft) in the home. It may flower and produce fruit in a conservatory (sun room).

Light Bright/filtered.
Temperature Warm/humid.
Watering and feeding Water freely, applying a balanced liquid fertilizer each time, when in growth. Water sparingly in winter.
Cultivation The large leaves will need a heavy pot to steady them. Grow in loam-based potting mix and pot up the suckers that appear at the base of the plant if you wish to propagate.

Phoenix canariensis
Canary Island palm

Most of the plants in this genus of palms will become small trees outdoors, but some make attractive indoor plants when young. This species has feathery fronds, stiff and erect at first, arching later, with narrow leaflets.

Light Bright/filtered.
Temperature Average room.
Watering and feeding Water moderately and apply a balanced liquid fertilizer monthly when in growth. Water sparingly in winter.
Cultivation Pot on only when the plant becomes pot-bound as it dislikes its roots being disturbed.

Soleirolia soleirolii
Mind-your-own-business, baby's tears

This spreading plant is used as ground cover in gardens, but forms mounds of bright green foliage if grown in a pot indoors. The tiny leaves are held on thin stems that give the plant a quivering, fragile look. It likes damp conditions.

Light Bright/indirect.
Temperature Cool to warm/humid.
Watering and feeding Water freely and apply a balanced liquid fertilizer monthly when in growth. Water sparingly in winter. Mist regularly.
Cultivation In late spring, divide the plant and pot on in a loam-based potting mix.

Sparrmannia africana
African hemp

This tree has hairy, heart-shaped leaves. Small white flowers appear in summer, but are often hidden under the leaves. The leaves look stunning with light shining behind them. This plant will grow up to 2.1m (7ft) tall in the home.

Light Bright/filtered.
Temperature Cool to warm.
Watering and feeding Water freely and apply a balanced liquid fertilizer monthly from spring. Water sparingly in winter.
Cultivation When pot-bound, pot on into a heavy pot, using a loam-based mix.

Ficus 'Ali King'

Musa acuminata 'Dwarf Cavendish'

Soleirolia soleirolii

Sparrmannia africana

Tacca chantrieri

Agave americana

Echeveria elegans

Kalanchoe thyrsiflora

Tacca chantrieri

Bat flower, devil flower
Weird and beautiful, the
flower of this perennial has
a complex structure. The
green, bell-shaped petals
are surrounded by pairs of
darker green, or black, floral
bracts and hung with long
"whiskers", thread-like
appendages that can reach
up to 25cm (10in) in length.
Light Partial shade.
Temperature Warm/humid.
Watering and feeding Water
freely throughout the year.
In summer, mist regularly
and apply a half-strength
foliar feed monthly.
Cultivation Pot on every few
years, using equal parts
coarse bark and leaf
mould, with added slow-
release fertilizer.

Yucca

Two species of these
evergreen trees and shrubs
are grown as indoor plants.
The leaves of *Y. aloifolia* grow
in a dense rosette and have
sharp points. A pronounced
trunk gives it a tree-like shape.
Y. elephantipes is similar, but
the leaf tips are not sharp.

Light Bright/filtered.
Temperature Cool.
Watering and feeding Water
freely when in growth and
sparingly in winter. Apply a
balanced liquid fertilizer
monthly in summer.
Cultivation Repot small
plants in a loam-based
potting mix, if necessary,
and top-dress large plants.

Cacti and Succulents

Agave

Some species of this succulent
can grow enormous in the
wild, but they will remain
a manageable size in pots.
Mature plants may produce
flower spikes indoors, but
they are generally regarded
as foliage plants. *A. americana*
has large, blue-grey, lance-
shaped leaves, with sharp
spines. As a pot plant, it is
usually grown in one of its
variegated forms, such as
'Marginata' and 'Variegata'.
A. victoriae-reginae, which
has dull green, white-edged,
triangular leaves, is one of
the best to grow indoors.

Light Bright/filtered.
Temperature Cool to warm.
Watering and feeding Keep
moist when in growth and
reduce watering in winter.
Never let the potting mix
become waterlogged. Apply
a liquid fertilizer occasionally
during summer.
Cultivation Pot on in spring,
using a free-draining, slightly
acid potting mix with some
added grit and sand.

Dudleya pulverulenta

This beautiful rosette-
forming succulent is a
delicate greenish grey. The
tapering leaves emerge from
a thick stem. Red to yellow,
star-shaped flowers may
appear in spring or early
summer.
Light Bright/filtered.
Temperature Warm.
Watering and feeding Water
moderately and apply a
half-strength balanced liquid
fertilizer monthly when in
growth. Keep barely moist
in summer when the plant
is semi-dormant.
Cultivation Pot on in spring,
using a standard cactus
potting mix.

Echeveria

These rosette-forming
succulents are grown mainly
for their attractive shape
and colouring. Most species
will flower, and although
the flowers are not very
beautiful, they are sufficiently
appealing in most species
to be a bonus. Of the many
species and hybrids, the
ones listed here are just
examples. *E. elegans* has
fleshy, bluish-white leaves,
up to 15cm (6in) across.
Pink or red flowers, tipped
with yellow, appear from
early spring to mid-summer.
E. 'Perle von Nürnberg' has
grey-pink colouring.
Light Bright/filtered.
Temperature Average room.
Watering and feeding Water
moderately when in growth
and keep barely moist in
winter. Avoid getting water
on the leaves as this may
damage their waxy layer
and lead to rotting. Apply
a half-strength balanced
liquid fertilizer monthly
when in growth.
Cultivation Pot on in spring,
using a standard cactus
potting mix.

Kalanchoe thyrsiflora

The pale green, oval leaves of this bushy, white-frosted succulent have smudged red margins. It produces panicles of little yellow flowers in spring. The whole plant looks like a beautiful flower made from marzipan.

Light Bright/filtered.

Temperature Warm, dry, average room.

Watering and feeding Water moderately and apply a balanced liquid fertilizer monthly when in growth. Water sparingly in winter. Do not splash the leaves with water because it will mark them.

Cultivation Pot on at any time of year, using a loam-based potting mix with added grit in order to improve drainage.

Lithops

Living stone, stone plant These intriguing, dwarf, stemless succulents from southern Africa look like greenish-brown stones with a smooth surface. The pairs of fused, swollen leaves grow into small clumps. The pairs of leaves part to produce a single flower in late summer. Many species are available, but you are most likely to find *L. bella*, which has brownish-yellow, fused leaves with depressed, darker patches. White, daisy-like flowers appear in late summer or early autumn. Planted in a shallow tray that is top-dressed with gravel and small stones, it is difficult to distinguish the real stones from the living ones.

Light Bright/filtered.

Temperature Warm, dry, average room.

Watering and feeding Water with great care, only moderately in summer and not at all in winter. Start watering again when the new leaves appear. Feeding is seldom necessary, but if the plant has been in the same pot for many years, feed occasionally with a cactus fertilizer.

Cultivation Grow in cactus potting mix with added leaf mould. Provide good drainage.

Mammillaria zeilmanniana

These cacti are undemanding plants for year-round interest and will make you smile. The clustering round stems produce white, hair-like spines that are tempting to touch, but don't. It may flower in summer.

Light Bright/filtered.

Temperature Warm.

Watering and feeding Water moderately and apply a balanced liquid fertilizer monthly in summer. Keep almost dry in winter.

Cultivation Grow in standard cactus potting mix.

Opuntia

This is a large genus of more than 200 cacti, ranging from low ground-cover to tree-sized plants, many popular with collectors. The prickly pear (*O. ficus-indica*) is one of the most well-loved and sculptural of cacti, with its fascinating collection of prickly discs. The bristles can become lodged in the skin and are then difficult to remove.

Light Bright/filtered.

Temperature Warm.

Watering and feeding Water moderately when in growth and sparingly during winter. Apply a weak fertilizer, or one formulated for cacti, a few times in summer.

Cultivation Grow in standard cactus potting mix.

Rebutia fiebrigii

These cacti originate from northern Argentina and parts of Bolivia. This species is a compact plant with dark green, clustering stems, bearing white, red-tinged, hooked spines. Yellow-brown or reddish-orange flowers appear in summer. Rebutias are, in fact, grown for their colourful flowers.

Light Bright/filtered.

Temperature Average/low humidity.

Watering and feeding Water moderately when in growth and keep almost dry at other times. Apply a weak fertilizer, or one formulated for cacti, a few times in summer.

Cultivation Grow in standard cactus potting mix.

Lithops

Mammillaria zeilmanniana

Opuntia ficus-indica

Rebutia fiebrigii

plants for colour and scent

For sheer exuberance or to lift the spirits on a grey day, the sight and smell of colourful or fragrant flowers is hard to beat. See the different effects that can be achieved with clashing or subtly complementary colours.

Capsicum annuum Longum Group

Guzmania lingulata

Pelargonium Ivy-leaved Group

Clerodendrum myricoides 'Ugandense'

Red

Capsicum annuum Longum Group
Ornamental pepper
The conical ornamental peppers are held upright on bushy plants. The fruits turn from green to purple to red.
Light Bright/indirect.
Temperature Warm/humid.
Watering and feeding Water freely when in growth and sparingly in winter. Apply a balanced liquid fertilizer every two weeks when in growth until the fruits start to colour.
Cultivation Grow in loam-based potting mix.

Guzmania lingulata
These exotic bromeliads, mainly from the tropical rainforests of South America, are usually grown for their showy bracts. Dark green, lance-shaped leaves form a funnel that holds water. The flower stalk is topped by bright red or orange bracts that wrap around tiny, yellowish-white flowers.
Light Bright/filtered.
Temperature Very warm/humid (think Andean rainforest). Provide cooler conditions in winter.
Watering and feeding When in growth, water moderately, filling the rosette centres. Water sparingly in winter. No feeding is required.
Cultivation Grow in bromeliad potting mix. Guzmanias have such small root systems that they rarely need repotting.

Pelargonium
Grown for their colourful flowers or scented leaves, pelargoniums are ideal for a sunny windowsill or conservatory (sun room). There are different groups in a range of colours, including Regal (single flowers in single or combined shades of red, pink, purple, orange, white or reddish black); Ivy-leaved (single to double flowers in shades of red, pink, mauve, purple or white); and Zonal (single or double flowers in shades of scarlet, purple, pink, white, orange and rarely yellow). As well as their showy flowers, pelargoniums have attractive leaves, large, bold and round or small and ivy-shaped. The Scented-leaved pelargoniums have small, single flowers in shades of mauve, pink, purple or white, and are largely grown for the strong aromas that are released when you brush against the leaves. Scented species include *P. capitatum* and *P. graveolens* (rose-scented); *P. crispum* (lemon-scented); and *P. tomentosum* (peppermint-scented).
Light Bright/filtered.
Temperature Warm.
Watering and feeding Water moderately, applying a balanced liquid fertilizer every two weeks when in growth. Water sparingly in winter.
Cultivation Pot on in loam-based or peat-substitute potting mix. Cut back in late winter/early spring. Dead-head for more flowers.

Blue

Clerodendrum myricoides 'Ugandense'
Blue glory bower
This evergreen climber from West Africa is best grown in a conservatory (sun room). It has blue to purple flowers with long lower "lips". The winding stems can be trained around a hoop. *C. thomsoniae* can be grown indoors, but also prefers a conservatory. It has dark green, heart-shaped leaves and red and white flowers in summer.
Light Bright/indirect.
Temperature Warm.
Watering and feeding Water freely and apply a balanced liquid fertilizer monthly when in growth. Water sparingly in winter.
Cultivation When pot-bound, pot on in loam-based potting mix. Dead-head regularly to produce more flowers.

Lavandula Lavender
Aromatic evergreen shrubs with grey-green leaves and mauve, pink or white flowers. They are garden plants, but can be brought inside for a while or overwintered in a conservatory (sun room). *L. angustifolia* 'Munstead' has spikes of purple-blue flowers.
Light Bright/filtered.
Temperature Cool to warm.
Watering and feeding Water moderately and apply a balanced liquid fertilizer monthly when in growth. Water sparingly in winter.
Cultivation Grow in a loam-based potting mix with added grit or perlite.

Plumbago auriculata
Cape leadwort
This evergreen conservatory (sun room) climber from South Africa has clusters of pale blue flowers. There is a white variety, *P. a.* var. *alba*.
Light Bright/filtered.
Temperature Cool to warm.
Watering and feeding Water freely when in growth and sparingly in winter. Apply a balanced liquid fertilizer every two weeks in spring and summer.
Cultivation Pot on in the spring, using a loam-based potting mix.

White

Hydrangea macrophylla
A shrub with toothed, deciduous leaves and ball-shaped flowerheads in shades of blue, pink and white. Mop-head varieties have rounded heads of flowers; Lacecap varieties have an outer ring of open flowers. They make large shrubs in the garden, but can be grown indoors while small. They are usually sold as pot plants in flower in spring, but specially treated plants may be available in bloom at other times. 'Veitchii' has white flowerheads set off by textured green leaves.
Light Bright/indirect.
Temperature Cool.
Watering and feeding Water freely and apply a balanced fertilizer every two weeks when in growth. Water sparingly in winter.
Cultivation Cut back the stems to half their height after flowering and pot on, or grow outdoors in containers or in the ground.

Lilium hybrids Lily
The bulbs in this genus that are grown as pot plants are usually hybrids. They have become popular indoor plants with the introduction of compact varieties. Most hybrids have trumpet-shaped or backward curving petals in shades of red, orange, yellow and white, usually spotted, mottled, or flushed with another colour. 'Casa Blanca' is a striking white variety.
Light Bright/filtered.
Temperature Cool to average.
Watering and feeding Water freely and apply a high-potash liquid fertilizer every few weeks when in growth.
Cultivation Bulbs are usually planted in a loam-based mix in autumn or mid- to late winter, depending on when they are available. Keep the bulbs in a cool, dry place, with the soil just moist. When the buds show colour, move to a warmer room, but avoid high temperatures, which will shorten the life of the blooms. Plant outside after flowering.

Lavandula angustifolia 'Munstead'

Plumbago auriculata

Hydrangea macrophylla 'Veitchii'

Lilium hybrid

Hibiscus rosa-sinensis

Eustoma grandiflorum

Mandevilla × amoena 'Alice du Pont'

Primula obconica

Phalaenopsis hybrids
Moth orchid
These evergreen orchids are ideal for a warm home. The arching stems of flowers will last for months, and may appear more than once a year. *P.* Allegria is a beautiful white variety.
Light Bright/indirect; no direct sun.
Temperature Warm/humid.
Watering and feeding Water freely, preferably with rainwater, when in growth and sparingly in winter. Mist daily. Apply an orchid fertilizer monthly when in growth.
Cultivation Likes to be pot-bound. If potting on, use an epiphytic orchid potting mix.

Yellow

Hibiscus rosa-sinensis
Rose of China
This is the only species that is grown as an indoor plant. It has single or double, showy flowers, with stamens on a central column. Colours include red, pink, orange, yellow and white.

Light Bright/filtered.
Temperature Warm.
Watering and feeding Water freely when in growth and sparingly in winter, but never let the roots dry out. Apply a balanced liquid fertilizer monthly in summer.
Cultivation Pot on in late spring, using a loam-based potting mix.

Paphiopedilum hybrids
Slipper orchid
These winter-flowering evergreen orchids make attractive houseplants. *P. parishii* has twisted, brown-spotted, greenish petals, which are pendulous, and a greenish-brown pouch.
Light Partial shade.
Temperature Cool to average; likes humidity.
Watering and feeding Water freely and apply an orchid fertilizer every three to four weeks when in growth. Mist daily. Water sparingly in winter.
Cultivation Enjoys being pot-bound, but, if potting on, use a terrestrial orchid potting mix.

Purple

Aeonium 'Zwartkop'
This tree-shaped succulent has rosettes of fleshy, nearly black foliage.
Light Bright/filtered.
Temperature Cool to warm.
Watering and feeding Keep moist when in growth and reduce watering in winter. Never let the potting mix become waterlogged. Apply a liquid fertilizer occasionally when in full growth.
Cultivation Pot on in spring, using a free-draining potting mix with grit or sharp sand.

Eustoma grandiflorum
The poppy-like flowers are in shades of white, pink and blue as well as mauve.
Light Bright/indirect.
Temperature Cool.
Watering and feeding Water with care at all times, ensuring the potting mix becomes neither dry nor waterlogged. Feed occasionally.
Cultivation These plants are treated as annuals and discarded after flowering.

Pink

Mandevilla × amoena 'Alice du Pont'
This twining conservatory (sun room) climber has funnel-shaped, pink flowers. The milky sap can irritate the skin.
Light Bright/filtered.
Temperature Warm (min. 10–15°C/50–59°F).
Watering and feeding Water moderately and apply a balanced liquid fertilizer monthly when in growth. Water less in winter.
Cultivation Pot on in spring, using a loam-based potting mix with some added grit.

Primula obconica
Poison primrose
The pale green leaves may cause an allergic reaction. Pink, white or blue flowers appear in winter and spring.
Light Bright/indirect.
Temperature Cool.
Watering and feeding Water freely when in growth and sparingly in winter. Apply a half-strength liquid fertilizer once a week when in flower.

Cultivation Pot on in loam-based potting mix with added grit or perlite.

Tillandsia cyanea

Members of this genus are air plants, but those grown for their flowers can also be grown in pots. *T. cyanea* has pink, paddle-shaped bracts, edged with purple petals.
Light Bright/indirect.
Temperature Warm/humid.
Watering and feeding Water freely when in growth, ideally with rainwater, and sparingly in winter. Allow to dry out between waterings. Apply a half-strength balanced liquid fertilizer monthly when in growth.
Cultivation Unlikely to become pot-bound. Use special terrestrial bromeliad potting mix to plant up offsets.

Orange

Nertera granadensis
Bead plant
These plants have tiny, bead-like, orange fruits and mat-forming leaves.

Light Bright/indirect.
Temperature Cool, average room/humid.
Watering and feeding Water freely and apply a balanced liquid fertilizer monthly when in growth. Water sparingly in winter.
Cultivation Potting on is not usually necessary, but grow in a loamless potting mix.

Strelitzia reginae
Bird of paradise
Resembling an exotic bird of paradise, the long-lasting, orange and blue flowers sit in a boat-like bract. Only the species described here can be grown as an indoor plant. The main flowering period is spring.
Light Bright/filtered.
Temperature Warm/well-ventilated.
Watering and feeding Water freely and apply a balanced liquid fertilizer monthly when in growth. Water sparingly in winter.
Cultivation Divide and plant root suckers in a loam-based potting mix in spring.

Scent

Gardenia augusta 'Veitchiana'
The shiny leaves contrast beautifully with the double, white, short-lived flowers.
Light Bright/indirect.
Temperature Cool to average.
Watering and feeding Water freely and apply a balanced liquid fertilizer monthly when in growth. Water sparingly in winter. Use soft or demineralized water and never let the roots dry out.
Cultivation Repot in spring, using an ericaceous (lime-free) potting mix.

Hyacinthus orientalis
Hyacinth
The pink, blue or white flowers are held on a single stem. Use specially prepared bulbs for forcing indoors; plant in a cool, dark place and bring into the light when shoots emerge. Keep cool until they flower.
Light Bright/indirect.
Temperature Cool.
Watering and feeding Water moderately when in growth.

Cultivation Grow in peat-substitute potting mix. Discard or plant outside.

Jasminum polyanthum
Jasmine
This evergreen conservatory (sun room) climber bears a mass of white flowers in late winter or early spring.
Light Bright/indirect.
Temperature Cool to warm.
Watering and feeding Water freely and apply a low-nitrogen liquid fertilizer monthly when in growth. Water sparingly in winter.
Cultivation Grow in loam-based potting mix.

Stephanotis floribunda
This conservatory (sun room) climber has scented, waxy, white flowers.
Light Bright/filtered.
Temperature Average room.
Watering and feeding Water freely and apply a balanced liquid fertilizer every few weeks when in growth. Mist occasionally.
Cultivation Pot on in spring in a loam-based potting mix with a little extra grit.

Strelitzia reginae

Gardenia augusta 'Veitchiana'

Hyacinthus orientalis

Stephanotis floribunda

plants for every season

Stunning plants from all over the world are now available to flower throughout the year, and are far better value than cut flowers. It is very therapeutic and satisfying to watch your plants grow and bloom through the seasons, knowing that you have nurtured them well.

Clivia miniata

Crocus vernus

Iris 'George'

Narcissus 'Tête-à-Tête'

Spring

Clivia Kaffir lily
These evergreen perennials have fleshy, rhizomatous roots. *C. miniata* has strap-shaped leaves and large flowerheads of funnel-shaped, orange or yellow flowers in early spring.
Light Bright/filtered.
Temperature Average room.
Watering and feeding Require careful watering to ensure regular blooming. Water moderately when in growth, but sparingly in winter until the flower stalk is at least 15cm (6in) tall. Feed from flowering time until early autumn.
Cultivation Pot on when pot-bound, as soon as flowering is over, in a loam-based mix.

Crocus vernus
Dutch crocus
Some cultivars of Dutch crocus have bold, funnel-shaped flowers in white, blue or purple. When grown outdoors, they usually open like a goblet, but in the warmth of a conservatory (sun room) or on a sunny windowsill they open fully.
Light Bright/indirect.
Temperature Cool.
Watering and feeding Water freely while flowering. There is no need to feed.
Cultivation Grow crocus corms in loam-based potting mix in autumn and keep in a cool, dark place until they develop a root system. Bring into the light for flowering. After flowering, discard or naturalize in the garden.

Iris
The iris grown as short-term indoor plants are dwarf bulbous species, including yellow-flowered *I. danfordiae* and *I. reticulata*, which has blue or purple flowers, depending on the variety. *I.* 'George' has dramatic, deep purple flowers from late winter to early spring. They look wonderfully stark in a modern container.
Light Bright/filtered.
Temperature Cool.
Watering and feeding Keep the potting mix moist.
Cultivation Plant bulbs in early or mid-autumn, then place outside. When shoots appear, bring indoors and keep in a light place. Discard or replant outside.

Narcissus Daffodil
Daffodils herald the arrival of spring. *N.* 'Tête-à-Tête' is a dwarf daffodil with golden yellow flowers. It can be planted in a basket for a traditional look or in a clear container for a modern feel. The paper-white narcissus (*N. papyraceus*) has strongly scented white flowers. 'Ziva' is suitable for forcing.
Light Bright/indirect.
Temperature Cool.
Watering and feeding Water moderately when in growth. Continue watering if replanting outside.
Cultivation Plant new bulbs in autumn in a loam-based mix in a cool dark place. When shoots appear, bring into a warmer room. Plant old bulbs in the garden.

Summer

Bougainvillea glabra

This vigorous conservatory (sun room) climber has clusters of floral bracts in white, pink and purple.

Light Bright/filtered.

Temperature Warm.

Watering and feeding Water freely and apply a balanced liquid fertilizer monthly when in growth. Water sparingly at other times.

Cultivation In early spring, top-dress large containers or, if necessary, repot in a loam-based potting mix.

Campanula isophylla
Falling stars

This trailing plant has bell-shaped, blue flowers. It can be grown indoors for a while, but a conservatory (sun room) is better.

Light Bright/filtered.

Temperature Cool/average.

Watering and feeding Water freely and apply a balanced fertilizer monthly when in growth. Keep moist in winter.

Cultivation Pot on in spring, using a loam-based mix.

Impatiens hybrids
Busy Lizzie

Masses of flat flowers appear at any time of the year if the temperature is maintained above 16°C (60°F). Blooms are mostly in shades of red, orange, pink and white, of which many are multi-coloured and sometimes double. The flowers of the New Guinea Group are usually fewer but larger.

Light Bright/indirect.

Temperature Cool to average; humid.

Watering and feeding Water freely and feed every two weeks when in growth. Water sparingly in winter.

Cultivation Repot in spring if necessary. They are easy to grow, so raise new plants from cuttings or seed and discard if they become leggy.

Olea europaea
Olive tree

This evergreen tree has an elegant form and is ideal for a conservatory (sun room) or a sunny room with a large area of glazing. It has silvery green leaves and little white flowers, followed by pale green fruit that eventually turns black.

Light Bright/filtered.

Temperature Cool.

Watering and feeding Water moderately and apply a balanced liquid fertilizer monthly when in growth. Water sparingly in winter.

Cultivation Grow in a loam-based potting mix with some sharp sand added for free drainage. Top-dress a large specimen in its pot.

Rosa miniature hybrids

These dwarf varieties of the garden rose are available in a wide range of colours from white through pink to peach, yellow, orange and red.

Light Bright/indirect.

Temperature Cool room.

Watering and feeding Water freely and apply a balanced liquid fertilizer when in growth. Keep barely moist at other times.

Cultivation Grow in a loam-based potting mix. Prune lightly in spring.

Spathiphyllum wallisii
Peace lily

These elegant rhizomatous evergreen perennials are grown for their white, arum-lily-like flowers.

Light Bright/filtered.

Temperature Average.

Watering and feeding Water freely and apply a balanced liquid fertilizer monthly when in growth. Mist daily. Keep moist in winter.

Cultivation Grow in a loam-based potting mix with added grit for extra drainage.

Zantedeschia aethiopica
Arum lily

Striking, elegant and easy to grow, the flowers are usually pure white, but deep purple and orange varieties are also available.

Light Bright/indirect.

Temperature Cool room.

Watering and feeding Water flowering plants freely and apply a balanced liquid fertilizer every two weeks. Water sparingly in winter.

Cultivation Pot on in loam-based potting mix.

Bougainvillea glabra

Rosa miniature hybrid

Spathiphyllum wallisii

Zantedeschia aethiopica

Autumn

Aloe ferox

This succulent is green with red-tinged spikes, perfect colouring for autumn. Scarlet-orange flowers are produced in summer.
Light Bright/filtered.
Temperature Average room.
Watering and feeding Water moderately through the year, but sparingly when dormant. Feed occasionally in summer.
Cultivation Grow in a loam-based potting mix with sharp sand or grit to aid drainage.

Anigozanthos flavidus

Kangaroo paw
Although it flowers in spring and summer when grown outside, in a conservatory (sun room) it can bloom all year round. The flowers are orange.
Light Bright/filtered.
Temperature Average room.
Watering and feeding Water freely and feed monthly when in growth. Water sparingly in winter.
Cultivation Grow in loam-based mix with added sand.

Brassica oleracea

Ornamental cabbage, kale
These variegated foliage plants come in deep pinks, reds and greens, some with creamy white leaves edged with green.
Light Bright/indirect.
Temperature Cool.
Watering and feeding Water freely and feed monthly when in growth.
Cultivation Grow from seed each summer.

Colchicum

Autumn crocus
These corms are known as naked ladies because they flower in early autumn before the leaves emerge in spring. *C. autumnale* has large, crocus-shaped flowers, in shades of pink. The corms and leaves are poisonous.
Light Bright/filtered.
Temperature Cool.
Watering and feeding Water moderately.
Cultivation Grow in loam-based potting mix. Place in a light position and leave to flower. Plant outside after flowering.

Cyclamen

It is the florists' cyclamen derived from *C. persicum* that are usually grown indoors. They are available in a range of sizes and colours, including pinks, reds, purples, salmon and white. The petals may be frilled or ruffled. The leaves are often marbled with white or silver. They can flower from autumn to early spring.
Light Bright/indirect.
Temperature Cool to warm.
Watering and feeding Water freely when in growth, reducing the amount after flowering. Keep dry during the resting period. Feed every two weeks when growing and flowering.
Cultivation Grow in a loam-based potting mix, enriched with leaf mould and some added grit. Keep dry when dormant, repot in autumn and water to restart growth.

Eucomis autumnalis

Pineapple lily
This late-flowering bulb is ideal for a cool conservatory (sun room). It has tiny, green-white flowers, topped with a tuft of bracts. *E. bicolor* has pale green flowers with purple-margined bracts.
Light Bright/filtered.
Temperature Average room.
Watering and feeding Water freely when in growth and sparingly when dormant.
Cultivation Keep the bulb dry over winter and then plant 10–15cm (4–6in) below the surface of loam-based mix with added grit.

Nepenthes Monkey cup, tropical pitcher plant

The leaves of these carnivorous plants have a midrib that extends in the form of a tendril to become a hollow "pitcher", ranging in colour from pale yellow to green or purple-red.
Light Bright/filtered.
Temperature Hot/humid (min. 18°C/64°F).
Watering and feeding Water freely. Apply a high-nitrogen liquid fertilizer weekly.
Cultivation Grow in a potting mix made from two parts bark, two parts perlite and one part peat-substitute.

Anigozanthos flavidus

Cyclamen persicum

Eucomis autumnalis

Nepenthes 'Director G.T. Moore'

Begonia 'Norah Bedson'

Hedera helix

Hippeastrum 'Apple Blossom'

Isolepsis cernua

Winter

Alocasia

Elephant's ear plant
These plants are perfect for
creating a tropical mood.
The spectacular giant taro
(*A. macrorrhiza*) needs high
humidity and warmth, so
a conservatory (sun room)
is ideal. The dark green
leaves of the Kris plant
(*A. sanderiana*) have silver
veining and a metallic sheen.
Light Bright/indirect.
Temperature Warm/humid.
Watering and feeding Water
freely and feed monthly
when in growth. Water
moderately in winter.
Cultivation Grow in loam-
based potting mix.

Begonia

Foliage begonias are
attractive all year round. The
leaves of *B. rex* hybrids are
brightly variegated in shades
of green, silver, brown, red,
pink and purple. The leaves
of *B.* 'Norah Bedson', a
hybrid of *B. bowerae*, are
blotched brown and green.
Light Bright/indirect.

Temperature Cool room.
Watering and feeding Water
freely and apply a balanced
liquid fertilizer at every
second watering when in
growth. Water sparingly
in winter.
Cultivation Repot annually
in spring in a loam-based
potting mix.

Dracaena

These palm-like plants have
striking variegation and a
bold outline. *D. sanderiana*
has oval to lance-shaped
leaves, edged with a broad
creamy-white band. *D.
marginata* has narrow green
leaves, edged with purplish
red. More brightly coloured
varieties include 'Colorama'
and 'Tricolor'.
Light Bright/indirect.
Temperature Cool to warm.
Watering and feeding Water
freely and apply a balanced
liquid fertilizer monthly
when in growth. Water
sparingly in winter. Never
let the roots dry out.
Cultivation Repot in spring
if necessary in loam-based
potting mix.

Hedera helix Ivy

Some ivies will grow indoors
as well as outdoors. They
tolerate low light levels and
prefer a moist atmosphere.
Light Bright/indirect.
Temperature Cool.
Watering and feeding Water
freely in warm weather,
moderately in cool
temperatures. Apply a
balanced liquid fertilizer
monthly when in growth.
Cultivation Grow in a loam-
based potting mix.

Hippeastrum hybrids

Amaryllis
This bulb is usually forced
to flower in late winter. It is
found in a range of colours,
including white, pink and red.
Light Bright/filtered.
Temperature Cool room.
Watering and feeding Water
moderately when the bulbs
are growing; keep almost
dry when resting. Feed every
two weeks with a balanced
liquid fertilizer once the
leaves start to grow.
Cultivation Bulbs prepared
for winter flowering should
be planted when available.

Unprepared bulbs flower
later. Bulbs planted in late
winter or early spring will
flower in mid- or late spring.
A soil temperature of 21°C
(70°F) is required to start
dormant bulbs into growth.
Pot up, burying only about
half the bulb. When the
stalk reaches 15cm (6in),
keep in a light position. Cut
off the stalk when blooming
is over. Reduce watering in
early autumn and allow the
leaves to die back. Keep in
a conservatory (sun room),
or outdoors in summer.
Start into growth again by
resuming watering a month
or two later.

Isolepsis cernua Club rush

This indoor grass, formerly
known as *Scirpus cernuus*, is
fresh and green.
Light Bright/indirect.
Temperature Average/humid.
Watering and feeding Water
freely when in growth;
water less in winter. Apply a
balanced fertilizer monthly
when in growth.
Cultivation Grow in a loam-
based potting mix.

plants for eating

If you enjoy good food, nothing can beat freshly plucked herbs, salad leaves, fruit and vegetables. A wide range of herbs will grow quite happily in a window box outdoors, while several can be grown indoors on a sunny window ledge.

Allium schoenoprasum

Aloysia triphylla

Beta vulgaris

Coriandrum sativum

Herbs and Salad Leaves

Allium schoenoprasum
Chives
This member of the onion family is an attractive plant, with purple or white flowers, as well as being edible. The hollow leaves can be used in salads.
Light Bright/filtered.
Temperature Cool to warm.
Watering and feeding Water freely when in growth and sparingly during winter. Apply a balanced liquid fertilizer from spring to autumn.
Cultivation Divide bulbous clumps and pot up in a loam-based potting mix with some added sharp sand for drainage.

Aloysia triphylla
Lemon verbena
This is the most wonderful lemon-scented herb, with lance-shaped leaves on long graceful stems.
Light Bright/filtered.
Temperature Cool.
Watering and feeding Water freely when in growth, but do not allow to become waterlogged. Apply a liquid fertilizer during flowering.
Cultivation Grow in a light, free-draining potting mix. Take softwood cuttings in spring or semi-hardwood cuttings in late summer.

Beta vulgaris Ruby
chard, rhubarb chard
This leafy vegetable is easy to grow from seed. It has red-veined leaves and red stems, which can be plucked when young and added to salads. Grow on a window ledge where the light can shine through the leaves.
Light Bright/filtered.
Temperature Cool.
Watering and feeding Water freely when in growth. There is no need to feed.
Cultivation Push the large seeds into pots of loam-based potting mix from mid-spring onwards and they will quickly germinate. Keep picking the leaves when they are small as the plants can grow quite large and then bolt.

Coriandrum sativum
Coriander (cilantro)
This pungent Mediterranean herb has cut leaves and airy heads of small white flowers. It is not a very attractive plant, but it imparts a distinctive flavour to dishes. Coriander used to be grown mainly for its seeds, but the lower leaves are now popular in a wide range of dishes. It is also used as a garnish, rather like parsley. The leaves can be picked throughout the growing season.
Light Bright/filtered.
Temperature Cool room.
Watering and feeding Water freely when in growth, but do not allow to become waterlogged. Apply a half-strength balanced liquid fertilizer when in growth.
Cultivation Grow from seed each year in a loam-based potting mix with some added grit to improve drainage.

Elymus

Mentha pulegium

Ocimum basilicum 'Purple Ruffles'

Rosmarinus officinalis

Elymus Wheat grass

The bright green young shoots of wheat grass resemble a perfect indoor lawn. Providing you keep clipping the shoots, a tray of wheat grass will last for some time. The leaf blades are used for juicing and are allegedly very good for curing hangovers.

Light Bright/indirect.

Temperature Cool.

Watering and feeding Water freely when in growth, but do not allow to become waterlogged.

Cultivation It is best to grow new plants from seed. Health food shops sell the seed or growing kits. Sprinkle the seed on a thin layer of potting mix in a tray, water, and then put into a warm dark cupboard until it starts to sprout. As soon as this happens, place in a bright room where the "lawn" will burst into life.

Mentha Mint

Mint is a large family of highly fragrant, flowering plants that have been used for centuries for their culinary and medicinal properties. Although there are many diverse species available, most are more suitable for garden use. However, two mints make suitable windowsill or indoor plants. They are Corsican or rock mint (*M. requienii*), which is a mat-forming, semi-evergreen species, with a very strong scent, and creeping pennyroyal (*M. pulegium*). The latter is said to deter ants, so it is doubly useful indoors. Both varieties are low spreaders with mauve-purple flowers, but they have different cultivation requirements.

Light *M. requienii*: shade; *M. pulegium*: bright/filtered.

Temperature Cool to warm.

Watering and feeding *M. requienii*: water freely when in growth and keep moist at all times; *M. pulegium*: water freely when in growth, but do not allow to become waterlogged. It needs a very free-draining potting mix.

Cultivation Grow in a loam-based potting mix, with added grit for drainage.

Warning *M. pulegium* should not be used during pregnancy.

Ocimum basilicum Basil

This herb has pungent, bright green leaves. It is said to repel flies. The purple-leaved variety, 'Purple Ruffles', has pink flowers. The dark leaves look good planted with other green herbs or with tomatoes for the perfect Mediterranean antipasto. Keep pinching out the leaves from the top to encourage the plant to bush out.

Light Bright/filtered.

Temperature Warm.

Watering and feeding Water moderately. Likes dry heat and dislikes humidity. Apply a balanced liquid fertilizer monthly when in growth.

Cultivation Probably best to grow new plants from seed. Likes a rich loam-based potting mix with some added grit for drainage.

Origanum Oregano

Pungent and aromatic, oregano (*O. vulgare*) and sweet marjoram (*O. majorana*) will flourish on a cool, bright windowsill. They are both widely used in Mediterranean dishes.

Light Bright/filtered.

Temperature Cool.

Watering and feeding Water moderately and apply a half-strength liquid fertilizer monthly when in growth. Water sparingly in winter.

Cultivation Grow in a loam-based mix, with added sharp sand for drainage.

Rosmarinus officinalis Rosemary

The leaves of this highly aromatic evergreen herb from the Mediterranean make it an attractive visitor indoors, perhaps to decorate an informal dining table, but it is really a garden plant.

Light Bright/filtered.

Temperature Cool room.

Watering and feeding Water as required.

Cultivation Plant outside after a brief visit indoors.

Fruit and Vegetables

Capsicum annuum Grossum Group

Sweet or bell peppers
The heavy red or green
fruits are borne on quite
delicate stems and will
need staking as they ripen.
Peppers require plenty
of warmth in order to
ripen; they make good
conservatory (sun room)
plants, or they can be grown
on a sunny windowsill.
Pinch out the tips of young
plants to encourage a good
bushy habit. Hot chilli
peppers (*C. annuum*
Longum Group) can be
grown in the same way as
sweet peppers.
Light Bright/filtered.
Temperature Warm
(above 21°C/70°F).
Watering and feeding Water
freely and apply a balanced
liquid fertilizer every two
weeks when in growth until
the fruit starts to colour.
Cultivation Grow new
from seed in early spring
each year.

Citrus

Both oranges and lemons
are probably natives of
northern India, certainly
China, and are thought to
have been brought to the
West by Arab traders via
North Africa, Arabia and
Syria, thence to Spain
and Sicily. As their origins
suggest, citrus plants
are tender and must be
protected from frost
in temperate regions.
However, they actually
prefer cool rather than
hot conditions. If they are
grown in northern climates,
with cold, frosty winters,
they can be kept outdoors
during the summer, but
must be brought indoors to
a temperate conservatory
(sun room) in the winter.

The glossy evergreen
leaves of the lemon tree
(*C. limon*) set off the small
white flowers beautifully.
The fruit takes a long time
to ripen and, in fact, the
plant will probably not
produce fruit until it has
grown into a small tree
with mature root growth.

Bitter Seville oranges
(*C. aurantium*), along with
other citrus fruits, are
beautiful, exotic plants for
a conservatory. Most citrus
trees may reach a height of
approximately 1.8–3m
(6–10ft) if they are grown
in a conservatory.
Light Bright/filtered.
Temperature Cool to warm;
they hate draughts.
Watering and feeding Water
freely when in growth,
allowing the potting mix
to partially dry out before
watering again, and in
winter reduce watering to a
minimum. Mist daily when
in growth and apply a
balanced liquid fertilizer
every three weeks.
Cultivation Pot on, if need
be, in spring, using a loam-
based potting mix, or
top-dress with fresh potting
mix. Try growing from
pips (seeds).

Fortunella japonica

Kumquat
Although the kumquat
looks like a member of the
citrus family, it belongs to a
different genus. It is a small,
compact, good-looking tree
which makes an ideal
conservatory (sun room)
plant. The glossy evergreen
leaves set off the small
white flowers to perfection,
and the egg-shaped fruits
that follow are a lovely
bright orange-yellow. They
ripen in autumn and
winter. Frozen kumquats
can be used to make
wonderfully exotic ice
cubes in summer drinks.
Light Bright/filtered.
Temperature Cool to warm;
it hates draughts.
Watering and feeding Water
freely when in growth,
allowing the potting mix to
partially dry out before
watering again, and in
winter reduce watering
to a minimum. Mist daily
when in growth and
apply a balanced liquid
fertilizer every three weeks.
Cultivation Pot on, if
necessary, in spring,
using a loam-based potting
mix, or top-dress with fresh
potting mix. Try growing
kumquats from pips.

Capsicum annuum Grossum Group

Citrus limon

Citrus aurantium

Fortunella japonica

Fragaria vesca

Lycopersicon esculentum

Rheum × hybridum

Solanum melongena

Fragaria vesca
Alpine strawberry

The strawberry is a creeping perennial with pretty, white flowers that have yellow centres. The delicious small fruit has tiny yellow seeds embedded in the surface. *F. vesca* has smaller, but more aromatic, fruits that can be eaten fresh or used in desserts, conserves and juices.
Light Bright/filtered.
Temperature Cool.
Watering and feeding Water freely when in growth but do not allow to become waterlogged. Apply a liquid fertilizer during flowering.
Cultivation Remove side runners between spring and autumn, and pot on in a loam-based potting mix.

Lycopersicon esculentum Tomato
Dwarf varieties of tomato are available which can be grown indoors. 'Minibel' and 'Tumbler' are both excellent varieties. Apply a thick mulch of organic matter to help retain moisture.
Light Bright/filtered.

Temperature Warm.
Watering and feeding Water freely when in growth and apply a proprietary tomato feed every two weeks.
Cultivation Grow from seed or buy young plants and treat them as annuals.

Mushrooms
It is possible to grow both button (white) and oyster mushrooms indoors. There are specialist mushroom suppliers who will be able to provide you with the potting mix, spawn and mycelium in kit form. There should be full instructions on growing the mushrooms. It important to mention that many people are allergic to the spores and, indeed, to the fungus itself. Remember that mushrooms need a well-ventilated space, away from living areas, so they are not really suitable for small apartments. It is well worth trying to grow some mushrooms, though, because it is very satisfying if you manage to grow a good crop.

Rheum × hybridum
Rhubarb

The architectural leaves and sturdy stems of this perennial make it a striking addition to the kitchen. Remove any flower stalks before they bloom in order to encourage the production of the leaf stalks. Rhubarb can be grown in a large container indoors for a short while, but then should be transplanted outdoors. Rhubarb would look especially smart in a large galvanized metal kitchen container. It is important to note that the leaves of rhubarb are poisonous. Only eat the cooked stems.
Light Bright/filtered.
Temperature Cool.
Watering and feeding The soil must not be allowed to dry out, even when the plant is dormant.
Cultivation Although strictly a garden plant, rhubarb will be happy indoors for a while. Grow in a loam-based potting mix with added slow-release fertilizer granules.

Solanum melongena
Aubergine (eggplant)

These will respond well to being indoors, particularly if they are grown in a conservatory (sun room). In northern climates they are, in fact, grown in a greenhouse. Although not the prettiest of plants – they have sharp prickles on the backs of the leaves and tend to look rather droopy – aubergines are rewarding to grow. Good varieties include 'Kermit' and 'Moneymaker'. The fruits can be stored for a few weeks after harvesting in a humid room. Regularly picking the fruit will encourage the production of more.
Light Bright/filtered.
Temperature Warm.
Watering and feeding Keep well watered and add a mulch to the surface of the potting mix to help retain moisture. Feed with a balanced liquid fertilizer every two weeks.
Cultivation Grow from seed every year, soaking the seeds first for a day or two.

practicalities

Plants are really no different from ourselves in their requirements for a happy life. They need food, water, daylight and warmth as well as a little care and maintenance. Close attention to these needs will ensure they thrive and flourish.

light levels

Before buying a plant, think carefully about where you will put it because light level requirements vary from plant to plant. Good garden centres and nurseries will advise you on your choice, which will help prevent expensive errors. Read the plant labels and follow the notes on care, particularly on light levels and watering. Keep instruction labels to hand for future reference. Also, find out about the plant's natural habitat as this will give vital clues to the sort of conditions it needs.

Most flowering houseplants need good light levels, but will tolerate a less sunny position for a couple of weeks as long as they are moved back into the light afterwards. Garden plants can also be

above Orchids need plenty of bright, filtered light and high levels of humidity. Some orchids are remarkably easy to look after and the flowers can last for months.

brought indoors for a short time, while most indoor plants will benefit from a little warm rain on an outdoor window ledge.

Although artificial lighting can help boost light levels indoors, it in no way makes up for natural daylight. Most houseplants prefer bright, filtered, natural light. This means that they do not like to bake on a sunny windowsill and will need a little shade from hot midday sun. Garden plants are sheltered by other plants and their roots are buried in deep soil, but houseplants are usually alone in a small amount of potting mix, so they can easily overheat. Cacti and succulents are happy in full sun, as are some of the pelargonium family, but it is still important to watch for scorching because sunshine through glass is very different from sunshine outside with a soft breeze.

In general, flowering plants need higher light levels than foliage plants, while plants with dark green leaves need less light than those with silver-grey leaves. If there is too much light, the leaves will shrivel up and fall off or become bleached and pale. The potting mix will also dry out quickly in full sun and the plant's roots will be unable to penetrate the baked potting mix. A bright sunny window that gets afternoon sun, rather than stronger midday sun, is usually a good place for most plants.

Plants that like to be moist are also usually shade-lovers. They are happy in a more humid room, such as a bathroom, with indirect light. But they still need light, so use pale-coloured walls to reflect light.

temperature and humidity

Many houseplants prefer a daytime temperature of 18–21°C (64–70°F). In 'Plant Focus', this is referred to as average warmth. Some plants require a cooler temperature during their dormant phase in late autumn and winter. Centrally heated homes can be too hot and dry for plants, with radiators below windowsills making this area hot during the day and often chilly and draughty at night.

Plants breathe through their leaves, but they also lose moisture through them, so raising the humidity around their pots can be beneficial. A little water poured into a pebble-filled tray will raise humidity levels without the plant having to sit directly in the water. Grouping plants together also raises the humidity around them.

Conservatories (sun rooms) need good ventilation to prevent a build-up of heat and humidity. They should be fitted with windows that open, as well as some form of shading. Opening windows improves air circulation on a warm day, but can also let in cold draughts. Finding the right balance is difficult, so invest in a device with a digital readout, showing inside and outside temperatures, as well as relative humidity. If the air is too humid, mould will appear on leaves and drought-loving plants will show patches of rot. Destroy any affected leaves because moulds are airborne and quickly spread. Tell-tale signs of inadequate humidity levels are buds falling off or not opening, leaves turning yellow and drooping or turning brown at the tips. Containers of rainwater will increase humidity. Hand-held misters can also be useful; mist twice a day in hot weather.

above Standing plants in a tray of damp, expanded clay granules will greatly increase the humidity around them. Grouping plants together in this way also raises humidity levels, and is a good idea if you are going away for a few days.
above left Plants absorb water through their leaves, so misting can benefit some plants. Hard water can leave white deposits on leaves so use filtered or cooled boiled water or rainwater.

watering and feeding

Giving your plants the correct amount of fertilizer and water is crucial to successful plant care. Isolating a plant in a pot means that it cannot search deep down for nutrients and water, as it would in the ground, while water will also drain away less quickly.

Watering

Spring and summer are the growing seasons for most plants. During this time, they need regular water to produce new shoots and flowers. They rest in autumn and winter and need less water, just enough to keep the potting mix from drying out. Over-watering is the commonest cause of death for many plants.

Many plants dislike hard tapwater, especially the lime-haters, such as gardenias. Ideally, you should use rainwater for these plants, but, if this is difficult, use cooled boiled water or filtered water. When using tapwater, always allow it to sit in the watering can until it has reached room temperature. This will prevent it from shocking the plants and allow substances such as chlorine and fluoride to escape. There are a number of different ways of watering, which are outlined below.

Top watering Water from above using a small, long-spouted watering can, avoiding the leaves and directing the spout at the soil.

above left Watering from below is the most reliable method to ensure that the water is absorbed by the potting mix, and is also good for plants that might be damaged by being splashed.

above centre Watering from above is the most obvious way to water, but try not to splash the leaves and flowers. This indoor watering can has a small enough spout to allow the flow of water to be directed on to the potting mix.

above right Fill the funnel-shaped cone of bromeliads with water. Spray a dilute feed on to the leaves every few weeks, and never use hard water on these plants. Follow the manufacturer's instructions when applying a foliar feed.

Bottom watering Water from below, allowing the pot to sit in a tray of water until the potting mix has absorbed as much water as it can. Discard any surplus. This is a good way to rehydrate potting mixes that have become so dry that the water bounces off the top. If the potting mix has really dried out, add a drop of washing-up liquid to the water to allow it to penetrate the potting mix more easily.

Plunging the pot Plunge the pot into a bucket of water until the mix is moist, but not waterlogged; then allow surplus water to drain away.

Bromeliad watering Some bromeliads hold water in a rosette of bracts which forms a cone-shaped cup. Carefully pour a little rainwater into this, topping up the cone when it is empty. Mist the plant regularly.

Feeding

Fresh potting mix has added nutrients, but, over time and after continued watering, these are used up, so potted plants need an occasional feed in the form of a balanced fertilizer. Liquid feeds are usually sold in concentrated form and need diluting carefully. The feed should be applied when the plant is in growth or flowering. A foliar feed applied to the leaves works as a quick pick-me-up, but move the plants outside before spraying because the minerals in the feed can leave stains that are impossible to remove. Other ways of feeding include sprinkling a few slow-release granules into the potting mix when planting up or pushing a feeding stick into the mix. Always follow the manufacturer's instructions when feeding plants.

above left Although all potting mixes contain some fertilizer, the nutrients eventually need to be replaced. Liquid feeds are added to the water and applied at regular intervals, following the manufacturer's instructions. They can also be used as foliar feeds to revive exhausted specimens.
above centre Feeding sticks are a way to introduce extra nutrients to the potting mix in slow-release form. Push the stick right into the potting mix as near to the rootball as possible. If you use a feeding stick, you will not need to apply a liquid fertilizer.
above right Top-dress plants that do not need repotting, but have probably exhausted their old potting mix. Removing the top layer of old potting mix and providing a fresh new layer can be beneficial.

potting up and potting on

Most plants bought at nurseries and garden centres come in small plastic pots with the roots already trying to escape through the bottom. At some stage after you buy them, they will need to be potted on into a larger pot with fresh potting mix.

Carefully check all new plants before bringing them indoors. Gently ease the plant out of its pot and have a look to see whether there are signs of vine weevil, a pest that has become rampant in pots in

above Potting on a cactus is rather like picking up a hedgehog. Don't try to pick up the cactus by hand. Instead, make a stiff, paper collar with enough left over at each end to form a handle. Gently tap the pot to loosen the potting mix. Lift the plant out and place it in its new pot. Use a long-handled spoon to pack the potting mix around the rootball.

recent years. The plant may show no sign of disease until it suddenly flops in the pot and a colony of white grubs with brown heads are found to have attacked the roots or bored into bulbs and rhizomes.

Potting Mixes

Choosing the right potting mix is vital to plant health. Garden soil is unsuitable, containing weed seeds as well as pests and diseases that may not be evident to the naked eye. There are two main types of potting mix: loam-based and soil-less. Sand or grit can be added to both these mixes to improve drainage.

Loam-based potting mixes are more like garden soil, but are broken down into a fine mixture and sterilized. They usually contain added fertilizers and hold moisture well. Their weight will also help to hold the plant firmly in place and stabilize the pot. Soil-less potting mixes are traditionally based on peat, but this is environmentally unfriendly, so choose peat-substitute potting mixes. However, peat-based and peat-substitute potting mixes tend to dry out more easily. Once they have dried out, they are harder to rehydrate than loam-based mixes. The mixes will often have a numbering system to denote their suitability for different applications.

Certain plants need specialist growing mediums. Some orchids and bromeliads, for example, are epiphytic, which means they grow in trees. They feed on the rotting vegetable matter and bark that accumulates in the forks of trees, their roots in a loose potting mix that allows air to circulate around them. Specialist nurseries and good garden centres should be able to supply these mediums. Cacti and succulents also do better in a special cactus potting mix, which is very free-draining.

Potting On

Plants can be traumatized by being potted on, but will recover most easily if it is done in spring. To pot up a plant, choose a container that is one or two sizes larger, ensuring that it is spotlessly clean by scrubbing with hot soapy water. Fill the bottom of the pot with drainage material, such as broken pieces of old terracotta pot, small stones or pieces of polystyrene, covering the drainage holes. Cover with a good layer

of fresh potting mix and tap this down to remove any air pockets. Position the plant about 2cm (¾in) below the rim of the pot to allow space for watering. Spoon potting mix around the sides of the rootball and tap down again. Continue this process until the mix is packed firmly around the rootball, pushing down with your thumbs to leave a firm surface for watering. Water in well. A fertilizer stick can be inserted into the potting mix.

Mature plants may not need potting on, but will have exhausted their potting mix. Scrape off the top layer of old mix, as much as you can without disturbing the roots. Replace with fresh potting mix. Water in well with a liquid fertilizer or add slow-release fertilizer.

1 Cover the bottom of the pot with broken pieces of old terracotta pot so that surplus water can drain away freely and the potting mix will not become waterlogged.

2 Cover the crocks with a good layer of potting mix and tap down to remove any air pockets. Place the plant gently into its new pot so that it is about 2cm (¾in) below the rim of the pot. Take care not to disturb the roots too much when doing this. Remember to check for vine weevils that may be lurking underneath.

3 Fill in around the plant with new potting mix, tapping down again. Firm in well until the top of the mix is approximately 1–2cm (½–¾in) below the rim of the pot. Water in well and insert a fertilizer stick into the potting mix.

simple propagation

Plants are programmed to propagate themselves. As well as producing seeds, many plants have evolved so that a leaf or piece of stem that is accidentally broken off will root and form a new plant, if it lands in a favourable spot. Gardeners take advantage of this phenomenon by taking cuttings, using a variety of techniques to give the plants ideal conditions for taking root. The best time is in spring and summer when there is plenty of light and warmth.

Stem Cuttings

Taking stem cuttings will be successful for most plants, especially those that have soft stems. Choose a healthy stem, and, using a pair of sharp secateurs (hand pruners), make a clean cut in the stem to produce a cutting approximately 10–15cm (4–6in) in length. The cutting should have at least one good healthy leaf. Remove any other leaves on the cutting and trim the stem just below a leaf joint. Dip the bottom of the stem in hormone rooting powder and insert the cutting into a small pot of free-draining potting mix. Once the cutting has rooted, plant up in a new pot.

You can put some stem cuttings, such as those of ivy, in a clear glass of water and then place them in a bright place. After about a week or ten days, tiny, hair-like roots will start to grow. Make sure the water does not evaporate, and, when the roots have reached about 2.5cm (1in), plant up the cutting in a pot.

1 You can propagate succulents very easily by cutting off a stem. It is preferable to choose a stem that will not change the balance or appearance of the plant once it has been removed.

2 Dip the end of the cutting in hormone rooting powder. Make a hole in a container of free-draining potting mix with a pencil or dibber. Insert the cutting into the hole. You can plant more than one cutting in each pot.

3 Once the cutting has rooted and shows new growth, plant it in an individual pot. It will grow into a new plant.

Offsets and Plantlets

Plants such as cacti and succulents as well as bromeliads produce offsets or baby plants at the base. Once the offsets start to resemble the parent plant, remove them with a sharp knife and plant the offset directly into an appropriate potting mix. This should be kept moist in order to start them off.

A few houseplants, such as spider plants, produce tiny plantlets at the ends of the trailing runners, while the pick-a-back plant (*Tolmeia*) has plantlets on its leaves. If the plantlets already have small roots, then they can be planted up in potting mix. If they don't have roots, then they can be held down on the potting mix with a bent hair-pin or paper clip until the roots have formed and are able to anchor the plant down.

Leaf Cuttings

The larger, fleshier leaves of some succulents, such as echeverias and crassulas, can be removed and planted whole in a new pot. Let the leaves harden for a day or so after cutting. Using a potting mix of peat-substitute and fine grit, make an indentation in the mix with a pencil or dibber, lower the leaf cutting in and gently press the potting mix around the cutting.

Leaves that have a strong mid-rib dividing the leaf can be cut into several pieces horizontally across the stalk with a very sharp knife. *Streptocarpus* leaves are ideal for this treatment. Insert the lower end of each section in damp potting mix and put into a propagator or even a simple plastic bag. Keep in a warm, light place until roots appear. With stiffer leaf cuttings, such as those from aloes or agaves, the sliced segments can be placed three in a pot and angled away from the centre.

If the leaf has a stalk, remove the leaf, dip the stalk in hormone rooting powder and insert in the potting mix.

Division

Clump-forming plants such as mind-your-own-business (*Soleirolia soleirolii*) and arum lily (*Zantedeschia aethiopica*) can be divided. Remove from the pot and gently split the plant into two. Ensure that each new plant has lots of roots.

Begonia tubers can also be successfully propagated in late winter or early spring by dividing those tubers that have two shoots.

above Propagate begonia tubers by cutting the tuber through the middle so that each part has a shoot. Dust the cuts with fungicide. Prepare two pots with potting mix. Plant both halves so that they sit on top of the mix. Keep moist and plant on when new growth shows.

Sowing Seed

Unless you have a conservatory (sun room) or outdoor greenhouse, sowing seed can take up too much room and will probably produce too many plants. It is not really very practical for most indoor plants, but it is an ideal method of propagating cut-and-come-again salad leaves and other edible plants that are grown from seed each year. Large seeds, such as those of ruby chard, can be planted directly into pots as the individual seed is easy to pick up and handle.

Find a good-looking seed tray if it is going to be on show, and fill with a potting mix that has been specially formulated for growing seeds. Gently firm down the potting mix with the flat of your hand and make shallow lines in the mix with a pencil or the edge of a wooden plant label. Sprinkle the seed as thinly as possible into the depressions and cover with a thin layer of potting mix. Water in well. Place the seed tray in a large, clear, plastic bag or cover with a sheet of glass. Put the seed tray in a warm place and wait for the seeds to germinate. Once this has happened, remove the sheet of glass or plastic bag in order to prevent damping off. Leave the tray in a light place, but out of direct sunshine. Spray the seedlings with water and don't let them dry out. Once the seedlings are large enough to handle (usually when they have two strong true leaves), plant them in small pots to encourage good root growth before planting them into their final container. Handle the delicate seedlings carefully, and always hold them by their leaves rather than the stems or roots, since slight damage to the leaves is less likely to be fatal.

1 Fill a clean seed tray with a fine potting mix, specially formulated for seeds. Mark out shallow furrows with the edge of a plant label or pencil.

2 Sprinkle the seed thinly into the furrows and cover with a light layer of the potting mix.

3 Spray gently with a mister so that the seeds stay in their furrows, undisturbed but lightly damp. Place the tray in a large, clear, plastic bag and wait for the seeds to germinate. Remove the bag and leave the tray in a light place. Plant the seedlings in small pots before planting them in their final pot.

pruning

Shaping is probably a better word than pruning to describe the needs of most houseplants, but some vigorous plants do need cutting back.

Pinching Out

You can encourage some plants to bush out by pinching out the leading shoots, resulting in new growth lower down the stem. Tomato and pepper plants respond well in spring and summer.

Dead-heading

The act of picking off any flowers that are past their best, known as dead-heading, will encourage the plant to produce more. Their aim in life is to reproduce, so removing the flowerheads jolts them into producing more flowers (and so seed-heads). Indoor roses will last much longer if they are treated in this way.

Cutting Back

If a plant becomes too large, cut it back using a pair of secateurs (hand pruners). The weeping fig (*Ficus benjamina*) responds well to cutting back quite severely. This is best done at the end of the dormant period in late winter or early spring as it causes less shock. You can stop climbing plants, such as *Jasminum polyanthum*, becoming straggly by cutting back slightly after flowering and tying in wayward shoots to a framework of canes or wires.

above left Pinching out the leading leaf buds between finger and thumb encourages the plant to bush outwards rather than upwards.

above centre Removing dead flowers, or dead-heading, not only encourages the plant to produce more flower buds, but also keeps the plant looking good too. By regularly doing these little maintenance tasks, you tend to see other signs of stress and can act on them before they get out of hand.

above right Many indoor plants can become a little straggly in their search for light. Trim to a neat shape by cutting just above a leaf bud or pair of leaves.

problems, pests and diseases

Most problems are due to lighting levels, over- or under-watering, or wrong temperatures. Plants under stress become more susceptible to pests and diseases.

Common Problems
Prevention is always better than cure, so be vigilant and spot signs of distress early on.

Upper leaves turn yellow Often the result of watering lime-hating plants with hard tapwater. Use cooled boiled or filtered water, or rainwater. Try using a proprietary feed formulated for acid-loving plants.

Flower buds dropping off or not opening Caused by insufficient light and/or humidity, or lack of water.

Brown spots and patches on leaves Could be caused by too much sunlight scorching the leaves, by drops of

above By wiping the leaves of this fern with a clean damp cloth you not only make it look better, but allow it to breathe and absorb moisture more easily.

water on sensitive leaves or insects. Move the plant out of strong sunlight and inspect the underside of the leaves. If insects are discovered, try brushing or rubbing them off, or use an insecticide if the infestation is severe.

Leaves curling at edges and dropping off Possibly caused by the plant being in a cold draught, or by overwatering. Some insects can also have this effect.

Leaves with brown tips and/or edges The result of lack of humidity or being in too hot a window. Can also be caused by tapwater, which contains chemicals, so try using rainwater or filtered water, or cooled boiled water. Remove the leaves because they will not recover.

Wilting leaves A sign of either under-watering or over-watering. May also be caused by vine weevil, which feed on roots. If you find a bad infestation, throw away the whole plant immediately.

Sudden leaf fall Single leaves fall off all the time, but if all the leaves fall off, then the plant has had a shock – either extreme cold or heat or complete dehydration. The weeping fig (*Ficus benjamina*) is prone to this.

Rotting leaves or stems A sign of over-watering and poor drainage which encourages the mould to grow. Remove affected parts and spray with carbendazim.

Yellow patches between veins of leaves Can be caused by magnesium deficiency, which is easily treated by a dose of Epsom salts. Follow the manufacturer's instructions when administering the salts.

Pests and Diseases

Treating plants that have pest infestations or diseases with chemicals is best done outdoors or in a very well-ventilated space. Treat edible crops with organic controls only, and wash thoroughly before eating. Keep all substances well away from children and animals.

Aphids Tiny, usually black or green, sap-sucking insects that cluster around leaf stems and inside flowers. They leave behind a sticky substance, called honeydew, and spread viruses. Spraying with diluted washing-up liquid often works.

Organic control Spray with derris or pyrethrum or use a biological control in the conservatory (sun room).

Chemical control Pirimicarb.

Botrytis Commonly known as grey mould, this greyish-white, fuzzy growth on leaves and stems is caused by the fungus *Botrytis cinerea*. The spores can linger in the air as well as in old potting mix and pots, which is why it is so important to be scrupulously clean.

Organic control Remove infected parts, avoid cool, damp air and improve ventilation. Try to improve air circulation around the plant.

Chemical control A systemic fungicide such as carbendazim.

Mealy Bugs Small, pinkish-grey insects that are covered in a white fluff and sit under leaves and in leaf axils. They also excrete honeydew, which then attracts sooty mould. They often attack cacti and succulents.

Organic control In the conservatory, use the biological control, *Cryptolaemus montrouzieri*.

Chemical control Spray with methiocarb or imidacloprid with methiocarb formulated for use on indoor plants.

Red Spider Mite You will need a magnifying glass to see this mite and its white eggs on the underside of leaves, which have a yellow mottling. This can be confused with a magnesium deficiency. There will also be a fine silky webbing. The leaves will dry up and fall off until only the shoot tips remain.

Organic control Spray with insecticidal soap (fatty acids).

Chemical control Spray with imidacloprid with methiocarb. Throw away badly infected plants.

Scale Insects These brown, oval-shaped pests just suck plants to death, congregating around stems and under leaf spines and excreting honeydew. The fig (*Ficus*) family are particularly susceptible, but there are different scales for other plants.

Organic control Wipe off with insecticidal soap and destroy the cloth. There is a parasitic wasp which can be used as a biological control in the conservatory (sun room).

Chemical control Spray with methiocarb or imidacloprid with methiocarb.

Vine Weevil The adult is a brownish-grey beetle which bites semicircles into the edges of leaves. If you are not squeamish, pick them off and crush them. They are quite slow-moving and easy to kill. The unseen danger is the fat white grubs which are found at the bottom of the pot and feed on the roots.

Organic control A nematode, *Heterorbabditis megidis*, watered in when the potting mix is warm in summer can help, but it may not work in severe cases. Badly affected plants should be destroyed immediately.

Chemical control Imidacloprid. You can buy potting mixes that have been pre-treated with imidacloprid. There are also proprietary brands designed specifically to treat vine weevil.

suppliers

United Kingdom

Plants
Ann Miller's Speciality Mushrooms
Greenbank
Meikle Wartle
Inverurie
Aberdeenshire AB 51 5AA
Scotland
Tel/fax: 01467 671315
Oyster and other mushrooms;
growing packs by mail order

Architectural Plants
Nuthurst Village
Horsham
West Sussex
Tel: 01403 891772
www.architectural plants.com
Unusual and exotic plants

Clifton Nurseries
Clifton Villas
Little Venice
London W9
Tel: 020 7289 6851
Houseplants and planters

Dibleys Nurseries
Llanelidan, Ruthin
North Wales, LL15 2LG
Tel: 01978 790677
Unusual houseplants

Jacques Amand
The Nurseries
145 Clamp Hill
Edgware
Middlesex
Tel: 020 8420 7110
Rare and unusual bulbs

Jekka's Herbs
Rose Cottage
Shellards Lane
Allveston
Bristol
BS35 3SY
Tel: 01454 418878
Herb seeds

McBeans Orchids
Cooksbridge
Lewes
East Sussex BN8 4PR
Tel: 01273 400228

Rickard's Hardy Ferns
Kyre Park
Kyre, Tenbury Wells
Worcestershire
Tel: 01885 410282
Ferns, many rare and exotic

The Citrus Centre
West Mare Lane
Pulborough
West Sussex RH20 2EA
Tel: 01798 872786

The Conservatory
Gomshall Gallery
Gomshall
Surrey GU5 9LB
Tel: 01483 203019
Conservatory plants

The Palm Centre
Ham Nursery
Ham Street, Ham
Richmond
Surrey TW10 7HA
Palms, tree ferns
and other exotics

The Romantic Garden Nursery
The Street
Swannington
Norwich NR9 5NW
Tel: 01603 261488
Topiary and citrus plants

Thompson and Morgan
Poplar Lane
Ipswich, Suffolk
Tel: 01787 884141
Seeds, including salad leaf collections

Toobees Exotics
Blackhorse Road
Woking
Surrey
Tel: 01483 7975534
Cacti and succulents, air plants and
carnivorous plants

Accessories
Homebase
Nationwide branches
Houseplants, composts and accessories

Kara Kara
2a Pond Place
London SW3 6QJ
Tel: 020 7591 0891
Japanese pots and containers

The Plant Room
Barnsbury Street
Islington
London N1
Tel: 020 7700 6766
Contemporary pots and furniture,
plants and accessories

R K Alliston
183 New Kings Road
London SW6
Tel: 020 7731 8100
Plants, pots and garden accessories

Skandium
72 Wigmore Street
London W1
Tel: 020 7935 2077
Scandinavian designs

The Conran Shop
Michelin House
81 Fulham Road
London SW3 6RD
Tel: 020 7589 7401
Pots, containers and accessories

Woodhams
379 Brixton Road
London
Tel: 020 7346 5656
Flowers, plants and containers

Yeoward South
Space S
The Old Imperial Laundry
71 Warriner Gardens
London SW11 4XW
Tel: 020 7498 4811
*Furniture and lighting, glass,
ceramic and Mango wood containers*

UNITED STATES AND CANADA

Plants
Indoor Gardening Supplies
P.O. Box 527
Dexter, MI 48130
Tel: (800) 823-5740
www.indoorgardening.com

Burpee Seeds and Plants
www.burpee.com

Mission Hills Nursery
1525 Fort Stockton Drive
San Diego, CA 92103
Tel: (619) 295-2800
www.missionhillsnursery.com

**Molbak's Greenhouse and
Nursery**
13625 NE 175th Street
Woodinville, WA 98072
Tel: (425) 483-5000
www.molbaks.com

**Richters Herb
Specialists**
Goodwood, Ontario
L0C 1A0
Tel: (905) 640-6677
www.richters.com

T & T Seeds Ltd.
T & T Seeds Garden Center
7724 Roblin Boulevard
Headingley, Manitoba R3C 3P6
Tel: (204) 895-9964
www.ttseeds.mb.ca/

Accessories
Bitters Co.
513 North 36th Street
Seattle, WA 98103
Tel: (206) 632-0886
www.bittersco.com

Domus
The International Design Center
1919 Piedmont Road NE
Atlanta, GA 30324
Tel: (404) 872-1050
www.domusinternational.com

**Kuda Furniture &
Homewares**
388 Carlaw Avenue
Toronto, Ontario
M4M 2T4
Tel: (416) 463-4805
www.kudaimports.com

Pier 1 Imports
www.pier1.com
For store locations and shopping

Smith & Hawken
www.smith-hawken.com
For store locations and shopping

Sur La Table
1765 Sixth Avenue South
Seattle, WA 98134
Tel: (800) 243-0852
www.surlatable.com

Takashimaya New York
639 5th Avenue
New York, NY 10022
Tel: (212) 350-0100

Urban Cottage
3211 Cains Hill Place
Atlanta, GA 30305
Tel: (404) 760-1334

AUSTRALIA AND NEW ZEALAND

Plants and Accessories
The Parterre Garden
33 Ocean Street
Woollahra NSW 2025
Tel: 612 9363 5874
527 Milirary Road
Mosman NSW 2088
Tel: 612 9960 5900
www.parterre.com.au

also:
The Parterre Garden Warehouse
493 Bourke Street
Surry Hills
Tel: 612 9356 4747

Lintons Garden and Home
Cnr Nepean Highway and
Canadian Bay Road
Mt Eliza VIC
Tel: 613 9787 2122

Garden Elegance
150 Railway Road
Subiaco WA 6008
Tel: 612 9381 2197
www.gardenelegance.citysearch.
com.au

Harmony Garden Centre
450 South Arm Road
Lauderdale TAS 7021
Tel: 613 6248 6149
email:
harmony@tassiehomegrown.com.au

index

Page numbers in *italic* refer to
the illustrations

Accessories, 24–7, *24–7*
Aeonium 'Zwartkop', 18, 72, *73*, 132
African hemp *see Sparrmannia*
African violets *see Saintpaulia*
Agave, 58, 128, 151
    A. americana, *51*, 58, *58*, *82*, 128, *128*
        A.a. 'Marginata', *66–7*, 67
    A. stricta, *66–7*, 67
    A. victoriae-reginae, 58, *66–7*, 67
Aloe, 151
    A. ferox, 98–101, *99*, 136
    A. vera, 41
Aloysia triphylla (lemon verbena), 115,
    138, *138*
alpine strawberries, 119, *119*, 141, *141*
amaryllis *see Hippeastrum*
Anigozanthos flavidus (kangaroo paw),
    100–1, 101, 136, *136*
aphids, 155
architectural plants, 58–61, *58–61*, 126–8
arum lily *see Zantedeschia*
aubergines, 94, 118, *118*, 141, *141*
autumn, 98–101, 136
autumn crocus *see Colchicum*
avocado stones, 10
azaleas *see Rhododendron*
Azolla filiculoides, 94

Bamboos, 10, *10*, *13*, 18, 46, *46*, 61
banana plants *see Musa*

basil, *12*, 114, *114*, 115, 122, *122–3*, 139, *139*
bat flower *see Tacca*
bathrooms, 46, *46–7*
bay, 35
bead plant *see Nertera*
bedrooms, *42–5*, 43–4
Begonia, 19, 137, 151, *151*
    B. 'Norah Bedson', *103*, 104, 137, *137*
bergamot, 115
Beta vulgaris (ruby chard), 38, *38*, 112–14,
    113, 120, *120–1*, 138, *138*, 152
bird-of-paradise *see Strelitzia*
Blechnum gibbum (hard fern), 46, *46*,
    126, *126*
blue flowers, 131
blue glory bower *see Clerodendrum*
borage, 115
botrytis, 155
Bougainvillea, 16, 52, *52*, 74
    B. glabra, 135, *135*
box *see Buxus*
Brassica oleracea (ornamental cabbage,
    kale), 101, *101*, 136
bromeliads, 16, 52, 146, 147, 148–9, 151
bulbs, 20, 33, 43, 51, 74, 90–3, 98
Buxus (box), 105

Cabbage, ornamental, 101, 101, 136
cacti, 19, 24, 62–4, *62–5*, 128–9, *144*,
    148, 149, 151
Calendula officinalis (pot marigolds), 40,
    41, 73, 115
Campanula, 79
    C. isophylla (falling stars), *44*, 135
Canary Island palm *see Phoenix*
Cape leadwort *see Plumbago*
Capsicum annuum Grossum Group (sweet
    peppers), 118, *118*, 140, *140*, 153
    C. annuum Longum Group (ornamental
    peppers), 74, *74–5*, 118, 130, *130*
carnivorous plants, 19, 98
Chanel, Coco, 79
chives, 114, 138, 138
Citrus, 35, *36*, 52, 116–18, *116–17*, 140
    C. aurantium (Seville oranges), 140, *140*
    C. limon (lemon trees), 36, 116, *117*,
    140, *140*
Clerodendrum, 55
    C. myricoides 'Ugandense' (blue glory
    bower), *17*, *130*, 131
Clivia (kaffir lily), 134
    C. miniata, 134, *134*
clover, 39
club moss *see Selaginella*
club rush *see Isolepsis*
Cocos nucifera (coconut palm), 18
Colchicum (autumn crocus), 136
    C. autumnale, 98
colour, 16–17, 71–87, 130–3
conservatories, 52–5, *52–5*, 145

containers: choosing, 20–2, *20–3*
    scale and proportion, 11
Coreopsis (tickseed), 106, *106–7*
Coriandrum sativum (coriander), 114,
    138, *138*
Corsican mint *see Mentha*
crassulas, 151
cream flowers, 80, *80–1*
cress, 36, 112, *112*
crocks, drainage, 27
Crocus, 16, 90–3
    C. vernus, *90*, 134, *134*
cut flowers, 16
cutting back, 153, *153*
cuttings, 150, *150*, 151
Cyclamen, 44, 76, 136
    C. coum, 91
    C. persicum, 104, 136, *136*
Cyperus involucratus (umbrella plant), 46,
    47, 126, *126*

Daffodils *see Narcissus*
dead-heading, 153, *153*
design, 9–27
devil flower *see Tacca*
Dicksonia antarctica (tree fern), 61
    D. fibrosa (tree fern), 61, *61*, 126, *126*
dining rooms, 34–6, *34–7*
Dionaea muscipula (Venus flytraps), 19,
    84–5, 85
diseases, 155
division, 151
Dracaena, 58, 137
    D. marginata 'Tricolor', 58
drainage crocks, 27
dry garden, *66–7*, 67
Dudleya pulverulenta, 64, 128

Echeveria, 18, *65*, 128, 151
    E. elegans, 128, *128*
    E. 'Perle von Nurnberg', 64, *108–9*, 109
edible: flowers, 115
    plants, 111–23, 138–41
Eichhornia crassipes (water hyacinths),
    94, *94*
elephant's ear plant *see Alocasia*
Elymus (wheat grass), 30–3, *30–1*, 106,
    106–7, 139, *139*
epiphytes, 63, 148–9
Eucomis autumnalis (pineapple lily), 82, 83,
    90, 98, 136, *136*
Euphorbia pulcherrima (poinsettia), 104
Eustoma, 44
    E. grandiflorum, 132, *132*

Falling stars *see Campanula*
feeding, 147, *147*
ferns, 46, 52, *154*
Ficus (figs), 61, 127
    F. 'Ali King', 103, *104*, 127, *127*

F. benjamina, 61, 153
F. carica, *60*, 61, *126*, 127
F. pumila, 61
foliage: light levels, *144*
  problems, 154
  texture and pattern, 18–19
form and shape, 14–15
Fortunella japonica (kumquats), 116–18, *116*, 140, *140*
Fragaria vesca (alpine strawberries), 119, *119*, 141, *141*
fruit, 36, 116–19, 140–1
fuchsias, 52

*G*ardenia, 146
  G. augusta, 17
    G.a. 'Veitchiana', *34–5*, *84–5*, 85, 133, *133*
geraniums *see Pelargonium*
Gloriosa superba (glory lily), 52
gloves, 24
grapes, 52
green, 82–5, *82–5*
grouping plants, 10, 11, 13
Guzmania lingulata, 16, *17*, 130, *130*
Gynura sarmentosa, 16

*H*allways, *48–9*, 49
hard fern *see Blechnum*
Hedera helix (ivy), 82, 104, 137, *137*, 150
Helleborus (hellebores), 27, *44*, *104*
herbs, 17, 35–6, 38, 112–15, *114*, 138–9
Hibiscus rosa-sinensis (rose of China), 132, *132*
Hippeastrum (amaryllis), 104, 137, *137*
  H. 'Apple Blossom', *137*
home offices, 22, 50–1, *50–1*
humidity, 145
Hyacinthus orientalis (hyacinths), 16, *81*, 93, *93*, 116–18, 133, *133*
Hydrangea, 80, *80*
  H. macrophylla, 131, *131*
  H.m. 'Veitchii', 80

*I*mpatiens (busy Lizzie), 135
  I. New Guinea Group, *54*
Iris, 44, 73, 134
  I. reticulata, 15, *15*, 16
  I. 'George', *90*, 93, 134, *134*
Isolepsis cernua (club rush), 82, *82*, 137, *137*
ivy *see Hedera*

*J*asminum (jasmine), 52
  J. polyanthum, 17, 55, *84–5*, 85, 104, 133, 153

*K*affir lily *see Clivia*
Kalanchoe, 18, 64
  K. blossfeldiana, 74
  K. thyrsiflora, 18, *62*, 64, *128*, 129
kangaroo paw *see Anigozanthos*
kitchens, 20–2, 38–41, *38–41*
Kris plant *see Alocasia*
kumquats, 116–18, *116*, 140, *140*

*L*abels, 24, *27*
Lavandula (lavender), *16*, 17, 43, *77*, 79, 131
  L. angustifolia 'Munstead', 131, *131*
leaf cuttings, 151
lemon trees, *36*, 116, *117*, 140, *140*
lemon verbena *see Aloysia*
light levels, 33, 144
Ligustrum (privet), *48*, 49
Lilium (lilies), 33, 90, 98, 131, *131*
lime-green garden, *84–5*, 85
Lithops (living stones, stone plant), 18, *18*, 68, *68–9*, 129, *129*
living rooms, 30–3, *30–3*
living stones *see Lithops*
Lycopersicon esculentum (tomatoes), 94, 118, 122, *122–3*, 141, *141*, 153

*M*ammillaria zeilmanniana, 63, *63*, 129, *129*
Mandevilla, 74
  M. x *amoena* 'Alice du Pont', *52*, 132, *132*
marigolds *see Calendula*
marjoram, 114
mealy bugs, 155
Mentha (mint), 17, 35, 114, *114*, 139
  M. pulegium, 139, *139*
  M. requienii (Corsican mint), 35, *37*, 139
mind-your-own-business *see Soleirolia*
minimal garden, 68, *68–9*
mint *see Mentha*
misters, pump-action, 24
monkey cup *see Nepenthes*
moth orchid *see Phalaenopsis*
mulches, *18–19*, 19, *26*, 27, 36
Musa (banana plants), 11, 18, *18*, 52
  M. acuminata 'Dwarf Cavendish', 127, *127*
mushrooms, 36, 118–19
mustard and cress, 112, *112*

*N*arcissus (daffodils), 16, 74, 90, 134
  N. papyraceus, 17, *17*, 24, *92*, 93
  N. 'Tête-à-Tête', *73*, 134, *134*
nasturtiums, 94, 115
Nepenthes (monkey cup), 136, *136*
  N. 'Director G.T. Moore', 98, *98*
Nertera granadensis (bead plant), 36, *50–1*, 51, 133

*O*cimum basilicum (basil), 139
  O. basilicum 'Purple Ruffles', *12*, *114*, 122, *122–3*, *139*
offsets, 151
Olea europaea (olive trees), 35, *78–9*, 79, 135
Opuntia, 129
  O. ficus-indica (prickly pear), 64, *64*, 129, *129*
orange flowers, 133
orange trees, 116, *116*, 140, *140*
orchids, 43, 52, 79, *144*, 148–9
Origanum (oregano), 114, 139
osteospermums, 55

*P*achypodium lamerei, 66–7, 67
pale colours, 76–9, *76–9*
pansies *see Viola*
Paphiopedilum (slipper orchid), 43, 132
  P. parishii, *42*
parsley, 114, *114*
Passiflora (passion flower), 52
pattern, 18–19
peace lily *see Spathiphyllum*
Pelargonium (geraniums), 16, 19, *19*, 52, *94–5*, 98, 115, 130, *144*
  P. 'Attar of Roses', 115
  P. graveolens, 115
  P. Ivy-leaved Group, 130, *130*
  P. odoratissimum, 115
peppers *see Capsicum*
pests, 155
Phalaenopsis (moth orchid), *16*, 43, 76, 80, *80*, 132
Phoenix canariensis (Canary Island palm), 58, 127, *127*
Phyllostachys aurea (bamboo), *13*
pick-a-back plant *see Tolmeia*
pinching out, 153, *153*
pineapple lily *see Eucomis*
pink flowers, 132–3
Pistia stratiotes (water lettuce), 94
pitcher plants *see Sarracenia*
placement, 12–13
plantlets, 151
Plumbago, 52
  P. auriculata (Cape leadwort), 43, *55*, 76, 131, *131*
poinsettia *see Euphorbia*
poison primrose *see Primula*
potting mixes, 148–9
potting on, *148*, 149, *149*
potting up, 148–9
prickly pear *see Opuntia*
Primula Gold-laced Group, *32–3*, 33
  P. obconica (poison primrose), *20*, 104, 132–3, *132*
privet *see Ligustrum*

P. obconica (poison primrose), *20*, 104, 132–3, *132*
privet *see Ligustrum*
problems, 154
propagation, 150–2
proportions, 10–11
pruning, 153, *153*
purple flowers, 132

Rebutia fibrigii, 63, *63*, 129, *129*
red flowers, 130
red spider mites, 155
Rheum x *hybridum* (rhubarb), 38–41, *41*, 141, *141*
Rhododendron simsii (azalea), 104
rhubarb *see Rheum*
Rosa (roses), 17, 33, 43, 76–9, *76, 84–5,* 85, 135, *135*, 153
  R. chinensis 'Minima', 79
rose of China *see Hibiscus*
Rosmarinus officinalis (rosemary), 17, 35, *36, 115*, 139, *139*
rubber plants, 103
ruby chard, 38, *38*, 112–14, *113*, 120, *120–1*, 138, *138*, 152

Saintpaulia (African violets), 98, 151
salad leaves, 38, *38*, *39*, 112–15, *112*, 120–1, 138–9
Sarracenia (pitcher plants), *19*, *84–5*, 85
scale and proportion, 10–11
scale insects, 155
scent, 17, 133
sedums, *63*
seed, sowing, 152, *152*
Selaginella (club moss), 36, *37*, 49
shape and form, 14–15
slipper orchid *see Paphiopedilum*
Solanum melongena (aubergines), 94, 118, *118*, 141, *141*
Soleirolia soleirolii (mind-your-own-

business), *14*, 15, 18, 36, 49, *49*, 127, *127*, 151
sowing seed, 152, *152*
Sparrmannia africana (African hemp), 18, 58, *59*, 82, 127, *127*
Spathiphyllum wallisii (peace lily), 96, 135, *135*
specimen plants, 30, 33
spider plants, 103, 151
spring, 90–3, 134
stem cuttings, 150, *150*
Stephanotis floribunda, 17, 55, 133, *133*
stone plant *see Lithops*
strawberries, 94, 119, *119*, 141, *141*
Strelitzia reginae (bird-of-paradise), 16, 96, *96*, 133, *133*
Streptocarpus, 98, 151
string, 24, 27
style and placement, 12–13
succulents, 18, *19*, 20, 51, 62–4, *62–5*, 98–101, 128–9, *144*, 149, *150*, 151
summer, 94–7, 106–7, 135
sunflowers, *38*, 73
supports, 24–6
sweet peas, 16

Tables, 13, 34–6, *34–7*
Tacca chantrieri (bat flower, devil flower), 44, *45*, 128, *128*
taro, giant *see Alocasia*
temperature, 145
texture, 18–19
Thymus (thyme), 35–6
  T. 'Hartington Silver', *114*
tickseed *see Coreopsis*
Tillandsia cyanea, 73, *73*, 133
Tolmeia (pick-a-back plant), 151
tomatoes, 94, 118, 122, *122–3*, 141, *141*, 153
tools, 24–7, *24–7*
top-dressings *see* mulches
tree ferns *see Dicksonia*

Umbrella plant *see Cyperus*

Vegetables, 140–1
Venus flytraps *see Dionaea*
vine weevils, 155
Viola (pansies), 44
  V. 'Molly Sanderson', 44
Vitis (grapes), 52

Water hyacinths *see Eichhornia*
water lettuce *see Pistia*
water trays, 22
watering, 146–7, *146–7*
watering cans, 24, *24*
wheat grass *see Elymus*
white flowers, 80, *80–1*, 131–2
winter, 102–5, 108–9, 137

Yellow flowers, 132
Yucca, 128, *128*

ACKNOWLEDGEMENTS

Author's Acknowledgements

I would like to thank the wonderful all-woman team who managed to work with a complete novice author through a hot summer, with humour and patience. To Caroline Arber for her beautiful daylight photography (and equally beautiful assistants), to Charlotte Melling for her impeccable style and taste, and to Lisa Jones for her practical assistance. A special debt of gratitude is due to Caroline Davison who had faith in me and remained impressively calm, creative and unfailingly supportive over the duration.

Thank you too, to all those real men at New Covent Garden Market whose sophisticated humour and politically correct views make plant-buying forays at five in the morning an unexpected delight, and to Michael James for sublime leafmould. To Jim, whose arrival has changed my life, and finally but most importantly to my husband Stephen for putting up valiantly with painfully early mornings and exhausted evenings, for sharing our house with an endless stream of refugee plants and associated paraphernalia, and for his total confidence in my abilities.

Publisher's Acknowledgements

The publisher would like to thank the following for lending accessories and furniture for photography: Castle Gibson, Clifton Nurseries, Couverture, David Mellor, Jerry's Homestore, Kate Schuritcht, Loft, Maisonette, Next Interiors, Plumo, R. K. Alliston, Shaker, Skandium, Space Boudoir, The Plant Room, The White Company, Twelve, Twentytwentyone, Ume India, Wallace Sacks Lifestyle, Woodhams' and Yeoward South.

The publisher would like to thank The Garden Picture Library for kindly allowing their photographs to be reproduced on p132tl and cl; p134tl; and p135cr; for the purposes of this book.

The following items of furniture are available from Parma Lilac, 98 Chesterton Road, London W10 6EP tel 020 8960 9239; fax 020 7912 0882; parmalilac@aol.com: White laminate table and wooden Hans J Wegner chairs (p.37); brushed steel bed and perspex shutters (p.42); column storage unit (p.44 top).